CHORLEY
Through the 1950s

Jack Smith

CHORLEY
Through the 1950s

First published in Great Britain by The Breedon Books Publishing Company Limited, Breedon House, 44 Friar Gate, Derby, DE1 1DA. 1999

Reprint edition published in Great Britain in 2012 by The Derby Books Publishing Company Limited, 3 The Parker Centre, Derby, DE21 4SZ.

ISBN 978-1-78091-028-4
Printed and bound by CPI Antony Rowe, Chippenham.

CONTENTS

ACKNOWLEDGEMENTS

The photographs in this book have been largely obtained by advertising in local shops and supermarkets around Chorley, and from my own collection and that of friends. It is unfortunate that many of the pictures came with a 'date and venue unknown' note, and in these instances it has been necessary to approximate the date and make a reasonable assessment of the place and sometimes even the subject. No doubt there are many readers who will recognise the photographs and I would be grateful to anyone who contacts me through the publishers to fill in the gaps in my knowledge. The later 1950s saw me leave Chorley to serve in the Merchant Navy, as an engineer officer with the P&O Company, sailing to Australia, and for the last few years of the decade I spent much less time in the town. In many instances, conversations with former school friends and other contemporaries of the time have allowed me to gather much information on those 'missing years'.

I would like to thank: Relatives, friends and contemporaries for the loan of photographs and information; Councillors, officers and employees of Chorley Borough Council for information and advice; Chorley Central Library reference department for their assistance; the *Chorley Guardian* for allowing me to use photographs from the newspapers of 60 years ago, as purchased by readers.

Finally, special thanks for photographic work are due to Francis Turner & Son (Photographers) of Leyland and to Mr David Lewis.

INTRODUCTION

I F, LIKE the writer, you grew up in the Lancashire town of Chorley through the 1950s – even if for just part of that decade – then perhaps you too will recall many of the events that took place then. Or perhaps, while reading the following pages and looking at the photographs, you'll learn for the first time what it was like in that first full decade after World War Two. For those old enough to remember, some memories will be happy or amusing, others may be just the opposite. One thing is for certain: those of us who do recall how it was in the 1950s have, since then, changed as indeed the town itself has altered. After all, it was 60 years ago and more.

Over that time, Chorley has changed due largely to the building development which has created an urban sprawl. This work on the outskirts of the town continues in this area on the site of the former Royal Ordnance Factory now that this establishment has closed. A new village is being built here, between Chorley and Leyland, straddling the boundary between the towns. In addition to this, linear development along the roads is effectively removing the green areas between the townships surrounding Chorley.

Some areas where this building on green land can be seen are along Burgh Lane and Eaves Green, and en route to Whittle-le-Woods. Also, at Common Bank and Ackhurst to the west of Chorley, on the way to Euxton. Here, not too many years ago – and certainly through the 1950s – was good agricultural land. Today, Common Bank has become an industrial park, while around Ackhurst we have a supermarket and a business park.

At Common Bank Farm in the 1950s, the writer spent time helping out, bringing in the cows and assisting with their milking for Mr Harrison. During his schooldays in the 1950s, at Ackhurst Farm – which changed from the Gamebird pub, to a 'family eating house' – the writer again spent time generally helping out during haymaking or harvesting, on a site where new buildings now stand. In one of the fields, where the Chorley Building Society offices are now located, was a look-out tower adjoining an old bus. These had survived from the war years and had been used by the Civil Defence and Home Guard.

In those days, 60 years or so ago, it was not always hot sunshine, despite what some may say about the glorious weather we enjoyed at the time. If the weather was inclement, there were plenty places to keep dry, like the old bus mentioned above. But in the town, around my end, the Queen's Road area, we had many garden sheds, cellars, etc to explore, albeit mostly unofficially. There were not many garages in those days, of course, simply because there were not too many people with cars. But there were several former stables and coach houses behind some of the big Edwardian and Victorian houses in and near to St Thomas's Road and Southport Road.

These hiding places often had boxes and cases full of weird and wonderful things to examine. And, of course, there were the old air-raid shelters, like the big ones in Queen's Road and Coronation Rec, and in Devonshire Road where many a game was played contrary to what our parents told us – "Keep out of them shelters; you don't know who's using them!" Of course, we didn't really know what they meant by this, but we still played in them anyway. The shelter on the Rec was very special due to its depth and the long sloping ramp leading down to it.

We had to make most of our own entertainment and this varied depending on one's age. The games played in the streets of Chorley during the late 1940s and into the 1950s, especially at night when it was still safe to be playing out, were orientated to the poor street lighting which, largely speaking, was gas until well into the mid to later 1950s.

Of course, we had 'the pictures' as they were then called, five of them in fact, where we often would go, either with parents or with friends. Some weeks, two or three visits to the pictures would be made, depending on how much spending money one had got to last the week.

This might be five shillings or similar, and it might vary if you had a job delivering customer's orders from a grocer's or butcher's shop etc, on a bike with a big carrier basket on the front. I did some of this for Messrs Stones, who had a shop next to the Red Lion where the White Hart now stands. Or, there might have been a bit of extra spending money if you delivered newspapers, as I did from the newsagent's shop in St Thomas's Road.

The photographs in this book reflect many aspects of Chorley life in the 1950s and, like me, many readers will surely recognise contemporaries, particularly at events like local dances.

Regarding dancehalls, there were several in the town throughout the decade in question, although some catered for the older generation who would today be a great age if they were still alive. There was 'old tyme' and country dancing, and many of the dance venues were church club premises such as St Mary's Hall, but for youngsters there was also 'the Vic', up all those steps, over the Arcade near the Market. The Tudor had opened in 1948 and was well used by the older group of young people. The term 'teenager' had not yet been invented for the most part of the 1950s.

The Arcade – or, to give it its correct name, the Victoria Arcade – in question had a bookshop at the Market end, run by Mr Adam Barnes, while the Arcade's corner shop was owned by Messrs Sharples and was a popular clothier's establishment. Men and boys visited Mr Darlington's hairdresser's underneath the Arcade, where through glass panels in the ceiling one could see the feet of people walking above. Another point about the Arcade was that it was a good place to shelter from the rain!

Perhaps I should mention those dance halls out of Chorley which were also popular, like Rivington Barn and Highways Hostel in Balshaw Lane, which allegedly had one of the best sprung floors in the district. Then there was the Co-op Hall for dancing, but more of that later.

The church clubs were used by the mums of the time for whist drives, while our dads might have played billiards or snooker there. And when we were old enough, we also might join our local club. There we would aspire to own our own cue, carried in a case with our name on it no less. There it was, hanging in the rack at the club. We thought we had really 'arrived' and were grown up when that was achieved.

There was another place in Chorley where the 'real action' could be found in the world of snooker and billiards. It was a place where the staff officially had to keep out young people, but tended to turn a blind eye to their presence. The location of this exciting venue was in the basement of the Royal 'picture place', in Market Street. The basement snooker hall had a bad reputation but was always a draw for youths of the time, like the proverbial flies around a jampot.

You were always guaranteed a game of some sort down there, with perhaps a cash stake on the side. As you went down the steps to the hall, below the auditorium of the Royal, you emerged into a large darkened room where most of the light came from the direction of the green lampshades hanging low down over the large tables. The scene always reminded me of some rather grubby pool hall in an American gangster film. Even the characters using the tables looked the part, completing the image with cigarettes hanging from their mouths as they leaned over the tables.

The hall was renowned for fights, a few of which I was involved in and so can speak with some authority. These fights would usually begin with an argument, often concerning the game being played. Or they might relate to the gang element, because in the 1950s there were quite a few of these in and around the Chorley district. It was all pretty tame, I suppose, when compared with today's violence, but certain hardware was carried and used – and not always for self protection I might add.

As the argument and subsequent fight developed, someone would use a cue on someone else, and then two fighters would become four, then six, and so on, and cues would be used on one another. Soon a full-scale battle would ensue. It wasn't too bad getting hit with the thick end of a snooker cue – it was the solid ivory balls which hurt most of all, especially if they hit you in the face or on the back of the head.

There was, however, a chap in the snooker hall who was either in charge or who was a 'bouncer' – I was never sure which – but who lost very little time in trying to stop the fights as soon as they broke out and was thus kept pretty busy. He might have had a baseball bat, or something similar – perhaps a piece of four-by-two timber – which he used to break up the fighting. He usually went for the legs to 'drop' the troublemakers. This was most effective, especially if you were hit at the side of the knee!

Fights would progressively move back towards the steps which came out on Market Street, by which time rival groups were often fighting side by side against this seemingly seven-foot tall, 20 stone, plank-waving superman. Remarkably, no one was ever seriously injured in these fights. Perhaps a little bit of pride was damaged, and a few cuts and bruises sustained, but not much else. Some readers may recall those 'happy times', when you had to be able to wield a snooker cue both on and off the table!

To return to a more serene image, the Theatre Royal, despite being altered to show motion pictures, still retained its deep stage and the necessary ropework etc, for lifting scenery. The auditorium had ground-floor seating and a balcony, plus a second balcony above that, known as 'the gods' or, more commonly in the 1950s, the 'monkey rack'.

The 'monkey rack', as well as housing the cheapest seats, was also a place from which we were often ejected. Seated there, we were above the projector beam showing the picture and would tie bits of paper to cotton and dangle them in the beam. They showed up as shadows on the screen, there were cries of disapproval from the audience below, and the usherettes soon paid us a visit. It was great fun but we got thrown out for it – and the Royal was a difficult place to let one's mates back into once you were outside.

Apart from the pictures, snooker and dances, there was not a great selection of suitable places to go or things to do in Chorley in those days. Or perhaps I should say, places that were in keeping with our perceived 'image' – and there was a lot of concern about image at this time. If it was not the clothes you were wearing, it could be the company you kept.

As in most eras, people liked to fit other people into categories. On one occasion my mates and I went to the Ambulance Hall where old tyme dancing was in progress. As you can imagine, we were like square pegs in round holes, especially as modern dancing was so popular and we were on the eve of the rock 'n roll era. Thus, we did not fit the image of the relatively sedate goings-on at the Ambulance Hall. But we were gradually accepted and subsequently made many friends there.

Dancing was, indeed, the main pastime during the 1950s, so much so that there was even a time when, to improve our dancing, we went to lessons, either up at the Vic, or at a school in Colyton Road, off Eaves Lane. I recall having to buy patent black leather dancing shoes and then feeling very self conscious when wearing them. But we had fun taking the mickey out of each other.

So far I've mentioned local dance halls, but there were times when we travelled some distances to go dancing. For instance, there were the Saturday evening train trips to Blackpool, for dancing at the Tower or Winter Gardens. I recall the platform at Chorley

Railway Station being so full of young people going to Blackpool for a night's dancing that it looked like the start of the town's holiday week. Incidentally, trains returning from Blackpool were nicknamed 'Passion Wagons' – but that is another story!

Another popular venue for dancing and which involved a journey by public transport was to the Riverside at Banks – transport to get there was almost non-existent – it was Bolton's Palais. There were some long queues for the 122 bus on Chorley bus station because the Palais was good for finding partners and there always seemed to be about the same number of both sexes at dances there.

As to Blackpool, I've always thought how lucky we are to live in Chorley, only an hour or so away from a place so full of entertainment. I believe many of us living in this area formed a close relationship with Blackpool because from a very early age we went there for holidays with parents during the post-war years into the 1950s.

Chorley's annual holiday period was Wakes Weeks. There was full employment in the town in those days with a large number of cotton mills, all of which closed down for Wakes Weeks, leaving Chorley almost like a ghost town, dead and empty.

Today, when holidays are staggered so much, it is difficult to imagine that a whole town could virtually close down for a fortnight so that everyone could go on holiday. In the 1950s, however, this mass exodus and the subsequent prevailing quiet around the town could be a little uncanny and you almost felt as if you had to creep around the streets of the town. A few miles away, on the beaches and in the streets of Blackpool, holidaymakers saw plenty of familiar faces – their neighbours from back home!

A week's seaside holiday would cost in the region of £10 per person, or less, for full board. Butlin's Holiday Camps were popular, but it seemed to take an age to get to them by train.

Of course, not everyone went away for the week. Some chose to have a stay-at-home holiday, going on coach trips each day – and coaches were still called charabancs (pronounced 'sharabangs') in those days. Many streets and clubs in the town would hire coaches for private trips which were like big family outings. Coach boots were filled with partly rusty buckets and spades, survivors from previous years' holidays – there were no plastic buckets and spades then – and if the kitchen sink didn't quite go, then there were plenty of crates of beer, particularly if it was a club or pub trip.

The 1950s were certainly the heyday of coach outings. They were convenient and reasonably cheap – and they brought you back home again at the end of the day. A lot of people complained, "I can't sleep in a strange bed," so the coach outings were ideal.

Another popular way to spend the holidays used trains for set periods, such as for three days or a full week. The system used what were called Runabout Tickets which allowed the user to travel for, say, a full week over specified areas of the railway system such as the Lake District, the Lancashire Coast or North Wales, all starting and returning daily from a local station.

To ensure one got full value for money, day trips would start as early as possible and return as late as possible. Sandwiches and flasks of coffee were sometimes prepared when one returned at night, ready for another early start the following morning. At the end of the week the day trippers were ready to 'go back to work again for a rest', as the old joke ran.

To those who were interested in steam locomotives, myself included, the 1950s was a good time to be a train-spotter. In Chorley, a favourite place to watch trains was at Rylands Crossing, at the end of Dacca Street, close to the former Three-Cornered Rec and Parish Church Girls' School in Bengal Street.

The crossing was replaced by a bridge in 2011. It was a good place for spotting trains, from Preston to Blackpool in one direction, and Chorley to Manchester in the other. Some 25 yards away was another set of lines, which were at a higher level and which carried trains towards Blackburn or Wigan. We were thus able to watch trains on two sets of lines at once.

Another of the changes within the town today concerns the former Blackburn railway line mentioned in the previous paragraph. Today, it is hard to believe that a line to Blackburn ever existed, yet it was much used by local people to travel the short distance to Heapey Railway Station, from where they would have a drink in the pub there before walking back to Chorley, or picnic in White Coppice, returning on foot via 40 Steps and Temple Fields.

The railway crossed Botany Valley via a multi-arched viaduct which was demolished by explosives in 1968, prior to the construction of the M61 which also passes through Botany. The line crossed Harper's Lane across an iron-girder bridge. On the side of this an advertisement for a brand of 'headache powders', called Cephos. Thus, the bridge was referred to locally as 'Cephos Bridge'. That, too, has now disappeared, as also has the rising embankment from Chorley Coal Yard near to Stump Lane Bridge, to Harpers Lane. It is now used for industrial units and a walkway.

It was here that heavy goods trains travelling towards Blackburn had the assistance of another engine at the rear, a banker, to help push the train up the hill, for it was a steep incline where hard-working engines were truly a sight to behold. It is a pity that no photographs of the trains or engines on this line have come to light. Today, Stump Lane Bridge, a wonderful multi-stone arched bridge, has been partially covered by embankments and the Blackburn line arches lost to sight.

Many memories of the 1950s in Chorley are associated with railways because we used the train a great deal for work and pleasure. We got most of our coal from merchants who had their offices in the railway coal yard off Brunswick and Friday Street, from where the clanking of wagons being shunted, or of a hard-working engine, could be heard in the night.

Even the trains on the main London-Glasgow line, passing Balshaw Lane, could be heard in the night, if the wind was in the right direction. Then there was the General Goods Yard at Chorley, to the south side of the railway station, entered from Railway Street. Older people will remember the tall wooden warehouse here. In front of Chorley Station was yet another yard. This was for the receipt of wood for Messrs Haydock's sawmill located on Clifford Street. The goods yard here was partially covered by sheds in which the incoming timber, mainly from Preston Docks, was unloaded. Sawn timber was also stored here prior to despatch.

There was one other major building in front of Chorley Railway Station, the one latterly used by Messrs Stewart Longton Caravans. The original purpose of this shed was for the storage and loading of cut lengths of Balatum, or lightweight lino, which was produced by Thomas Witter & Co at their local factories through the 1950s and 1960s.

Besides train-spotting, there were fish to catch and this pastime got us into plenty of scrapes as youngsters. Often we would fish in places where 'No Fishing' signs were treated like invitations. Even Astley Park Lake was fished regularly. Then there was 'Duggie's', or Mr Dugdale's pond at Chorley Hall Farm – there weren't many places to hide there – or the pond belonging to Mr Clitheroe of Astley Hall Farm. This was approached with caution, via the hedgerows where possible, because Mr Clitheroe regularly chased us off his land with more than a little enthusiasm.

But it was the mill lodges that were the greatest draw for us, because most of them contained goldfish. Our biggest problem was that the mill bosses seemed to like their lodges to have this sort of fish. They certainly didn't approve of us fishing them out, but it was too tempting because we could bring the fish home in buckets and supplement our spending money by selling them to certain pet shops in Chorley, the owners of which didn't enquire too vigorously into the source of the fish.

Of course, the Canal was good for so many things, from fishing to swimming, and for rafting. We even had a go at making a strange sort of canoe from surplus aviation fuel tanks obtained from Messrs Hitchin's scrapyard at the bottom of Harper's Lane. One of the problems with this was that the 'canoe' was always overturning and sank very easily, hence we used it on the canal where the water wasn't so deep. We never seemed able to get the ballasting quite right.

These then were some of the things we got up to as young people. through the 1950s. Hopefully your appetite is now whetted for a journey back in time – to *Chorley Through the 1950s*.

SETTING THE SCENE

A LARGE number of Chorley people who are reading this would have been at school throughout the war years. Many of them, like myself at Hollinshead Street, would have been attending primary school. Some might have been at grammar or technical school. Comprehensive education was still a long way in the future.

To begin this nostalgic trip back in time by trying to recall what took place in and around Chorley during the post-war years poses a problem because the era was still overshadowed by what had happened in the war itself. Now, over 60 years later, those wartime memories are a little jumbled and vague. I can recall events from the last year of the war, notably sitting around the wireless set as events unfolded which would eventually bring peace. And it was this pattern of behaviour which continued after the war, when we then listened to the radio more for pleasure than for information. Of course, many popular radio shows continued well into the post-war years. *ITMA* was arguably the most popular and synonymous with wartime Britain. But there was *The Brains Trust* as well, and *Music While You Work*.

Of course, there was also the cinema. Weekly family visits to the pictures were normal, as were trips down to the local picture house with your mates as you grew older. At an impressionable age, we probably felt the power of the movies more than most. There were some memorable films such as *Henry V*, and those brilliant war films as well as documentaries made by the Crown Film Unit. And plenty of choice about where to watch them, too.

Until 1946 we had six cinemas in Chorley. They were the Pavilion, Royal, Empire, Hippodrome, Plaza and Odeon. It was the Hippodrome which closed in 1946, to become a live theatre, although not long after this it became the Tudor Dance Hall.

It was the grown-ups who attended dances when the 'Big Band Sound' was so popular, as epitomised by the American services band of Glenn Miller, and each Sunday night there were live concerts on the stage of the Plaza. But it was not only the sound of the big bands which was popular in those early post-war years. So, too, was serious music like the prom concerts – and, of course, the songs of Bing Crosby, and Britain's own Vera Lynn.

The post-war years were also a time for reflection on the recent past, which was often recalled with humorous anecdotes, a large number of which centred around rationing restrictions, or, to be more precise, the ways that rationing rules were bent.

These stories were usually about the 'black market' which inevitably developed in the austere days of the war and its immediate aftermath. It was simply a case of supply and demand. And the items most in demand were often mysteriously supplied by equally mysterious characters. Equally inevitably, legends and urban myths abounded over the subject of the black market.

My parents were quite friendly with a local farmer, who farmed in the Chorley Nab area. It was from his farm that strangely-shaped parcels would be brought, and we would be eating unusually large amounts of meat all at once. That was one area in which the black market operated, but there were many more.

Almost everything that was in short supply could be obtained in one way or another. Stories of how they were nearly caught, or complaints that the people who were supposed to be implementing rationing restrictions never seemed to be short of anything.

During the war years and afterwards, when many items were still in short supply and food and clothing etc were rationed, each person was allowed only a certain set allowance weekly. The system was governed by coupons which formed the pages of a ration book. Each time the purchase of a restricted item was made, the necessary coupons were removed from the ration book. And it wasn't simply a case of going into any old shop that took your fancy; each ration book holder had to be registered with a specific retail outlet.

Often there was simply not enough of certain items to go around and so it was a natural thing for many people to try to obtain more food etc, unofficially and without having to surrender coupons for what they were buying. It was also a time of make-do-and-mend, when children whose families were not well off wore clothes that were badly fitting, but that they would 'grow into'.

Ration allowances during the mid-war years were (per person, per week): 104g of margarine, 57g of butter, 57g of cooking fat, 57g of tea, 226g of sugar, 450g of jam, and 28g of cheese. In addition, fruit, biscuits, tinned fish and tinned meat were all obtained by coupons as well.

Clothing coupons were obviously used for the purchase of clothes, and there were many more everyday items which were in short supply such as shoes, shoe polish, razor blades, cutlery, combs, etc to name but a few. When all these shortages were considered, it is hardly surprising that so many stories about the black market flourished.

As children in school after the war, we talked about how we had to sit in air-raid shelters wearing our gas masks for some lessons, just to remind us that we had to be prepared, I suppose. Now, post-war, we played in those now redundant shelters. At my local school of Hollinshead Street, the air-raid shelter was located where the Council car park is today, alongside the Civic Offices.

There were two deep shelters in the part of Chorley where I lived, one on Coronation Recreation Ground, the other in Queen's Road. Of course, these were places that were out of bounds to us, at least so far as our parents were concerned, but to children they were places of great adventure, especially the one on the Rec which had a long sloping ramp down which we used to slide.

Another point of discussion for children was the local Home Guard, because many of our fathers had been involved with that organisation.

Then there were the places where fire watchers had their look-out positions, such as on the top of the Town Hall. One of the best places, we thought, was at Ackhurst, at the top of the hill where Chorley Building Society stands today. Here, a tall wooden tower had been built alongside an old bus which had a platform on the roof, and access to the tower itself. This was a great place in all weathers, where we could make a fire inside the bus if it was wet, or sunbathe outside in summer. This was on the land of Ackhurst Farm, which was owned by one of my friends' uncles. We spent plenty time here in the late 1940s and early 1950s.

Returning to my former primary school, Hollinshead Street, there have been a lot of changes in and around the area since my schooldays. Many of the old buildings have gone now, such as in Byron Street off Union Street, the main entrance to the school.

In Byron Street there used to be a car scrapyard which belonged to the garage of Messrs Hughlock Hindle. This scrapyard used to be a good source of ball bearings for catapults, until we got caught and evicted. Between the scrapyard and the school was an old works of some sort. All this block, down Byron Street, along Union Street, to Stanley Place, where there used to be a shop and bakery on the corner, next to the garage, is now occupied by the Civic Offices building.

On the Flat Iron or Cattle Market, the cattle pens were still in place during the early 1950s. They stood on the site where the Gas Showroom Building was built, which itself has now been demolished to be replaced by new buildings forming the exterior of the Shopping Mall.

On the east side of the school was Clifford Street. It is still there today, of course, but then houses stood on both sides of the street. I spent a lot of time in Clifford Street, for I had an aunt and uncle living there. When the street was cleared of its east side buildings in the 1980s, one of those demolished was a former well-known pub. It was especially known among the bowling fraternity, for it was here that bowlers came from all over Lancashire to compete in the top games of the 1950s. This was the Robin Hood, which stood a short distance from the corner of Stump Lane.

The schoolyard emerged, as it does today, adjacent to Hollinshead Street Chapel, in Hollinshead Street itself. But in those days the scene was greatly different to what it is today. Across from the school gates were small terraced cottages which ran from opposite the end of Fellery Street, to the corner of Hollinshead Street and Clifford Street.

There was a single passageway in the terraced row, almost opposite the school gates. This allowed wagons to access the coke yard behind these cottages, and behind the cottages to the west side of Bengal Street, and bounded by Water Street was the Chorley Gasworks.

Great stacks of coke were piled in the yard, and spilled down to the lower level of Water Street itself. To us, these scree-like slopes were as good as a sledge run, and available any time of year. We used the slopes, riding on sheets of corrugated iron, or plywood, taking risks as we slid down. It was dangerous all right and we often ended up with cuts and scrapes from the sharp coke, but the slides were exhilarating and fast.

To the left of the school gates was Hollinshead House, a former early 19th-century house, which was believed to have been associated with the family of Hollinshead itself. This building was demolished in the 1950s. It adjoined the printing works which extends to the end of Fellery Street. In fact, the window lintels and brickwork of that building and the former Hollinshead House were of the same style and probably contemporary.

Bengal Street had small houses on each side, in continuous long terraced rows. At the side nearest to the Gas Works was a narrow passage way which led to more houses behind. These were of the back-to-back type, piles of coke almost surrounding them, and fumes from the gasworks often making the houses difficult to live in.

It was a street which we often walked along from school, carrying our gardening tools, for we had a school garden in Dacca Street, near the Three-Cornered Rec, which was next to the Parish Church Girls' School. My own garden plot was just about where the middle of the southbound carriageway of the town centre bypass is today, as it passes Halford's store.

There are so many other changes. The old property which projected from Stump Lane into Bengal Street, and just up Stump Lane to the left-hand side, before the railway bridge, was the town's 'Destructor' in Town Yard, where the old 'Big Lamp' standard finished up after it was removed from the corner of Pall Mall and Market Street.

Across from Byron Street, at the corner of the Flat Iron, was Chorley Baths where we learned to swim, with lessons first period on a Monday morning. The baths have been relocated to Water Street.

This, then, describes how it used to be around the Hollinshead Street area of Chorley in the late 1940s and early 1950s. It was certainly an area which, as far as we boys were concerned at the time, had a lot going for it.

THE EVE OF THE 1950S

THOSE readers still at school in Chorley at the end of the 1940s may recall how there seemed to be an upsurge in children's health care, and that the 'nit nurse' seemed to be visiting schools more often. And when the nurse found what she was looking for in a child's hair, then how that child suffered at the hands of their fellow pupils. Oh, the disgrace!

This increase in school visits followed the fledgling National Health Service which had been introduced on 5 July 1948. This was the time when the Government promised to look after us from the cradle to the grave.

There were also the visits for dental examinations to the School Clinic which was located on the Town Hall Square. I was terrified of these visits, and I was not on my own either. The dental care which we got in those days, was nothing like the care we get today. I'm not 100 per cent sure, but I think the drill used by the dentist was driven by a foot treadle. If it wasn't, it certainly felt like it, because the drill seemed to vary in speed and when pressure was applied to the drill, it slowed down and it felt like the tooth was being scraped out instead of being drilled.

Then there was the introduction of what became known as comprehensive education which was supposed to cater for pupils after their primary school education, irrespective of their educational ability and as opposed to the 11-plus examination which determined whether one would go on to a grammar or technical school, or stay at primary until leaving at the age of 15. Another of the educational innovations of 1948, was the GCE exam for pupils aged 16 years.

The nationalisation of the railways in 1948 was of passing interest to a young boy. My friends and I were train-spotters and spent much of our time at Balshaw Lane Station or at Iron Bridge in Charnock Richard which we would visit on our bikes. Here we would see the London-Glasgow trains being pulled by the grandest steam locomotives of the LMS Railway Company. These grand Pacific Class locomotives, pulling named trains, were in themselves a sight to behold, let alone 'copping' (seeing) an engine for the first time and noting it in your ABC. At times we were actually allowed on to the platform of Balshaw Lane Station, after being forewarned to behave ourselves.

We were even allowed on to Chorley Station occasionally, where we just sat at the end of the platform so that we could be close to a steam locomotive, and even at times be allowed on to the footplate for a couple of minutes.

Of course, being spotters we changed our venues from time to time, two such places being Back Lane and Bent Bridge at Leyland. It was here in 1947, during the steam locomotive exchanges between the Big Four railway companies, that we young spotters had the surprise of our lives when we saw steam locos from the LNER and the Southern Railways pulling LMS trains. Eventually the four big companies were amalgamated to form British Railways.

Another interest of the late 1940s and early 1950s was that of collecting autographs, although the stars visiting Chorley were a bit limited I suppose. My own autograph books were usually started off at school, when either very cryptic or suggestive rhymes were written in the books by one's friends of either sex. There was an exception to the visitors to Chorley, though, when actor Jimmy Hanley, famous for his part in the film *The Blue Lamp*, visited the Odeon.

It was the Lancashire Combination Football League which helped fill my autograph books in those early days, when we'd go to watch the games at Chorley FC's Victory Park ground and obtain the autographs of visiting players. At times we would go to the First Division games at Preston, Blackburn, Bolton or even Blackpool. Here, too, we managed to secure the autographs of several famous players, including the legendary Stanley Matthews.

Holidays, too, were opportunities to collect the autographs of the more famous visiting show business people. In Blackpool we would wait at the theatre stage doors, sometimes for hours it seemed, and then find that the star we were waiting for had gone out some other way. There were people like George Formby and Josef Locke. But I think the prize autograph in my own collection was that of the film star who played Tarzan, and perhaps the best of them all – Johnny Weismuller.

Back to the end of the war. In August 1945, American servicemen vacated Washington Hall which had been built as No.3 hostel for ROF workers in the war years, but was never used for that purpose.

That year also saw the first post-war General Election and one politician who came to address Chorley people was Sir Stafford Cripps, who gave his speech at the Hippodrome Cinema, as it was still called at that time.

The following year, Chorley saw its first street covered in tarmac – up to then all the streets in the town were cobbled. All the street lights were still lit by gas, however.

Between January and March 1947, during one of the worst winters that Britain had seen this century, there was a countrywide fuel shortage and mills and factories had to close. It was estimated that in Chorley, 4,000 local people had to be laid-off.

In April, the first ten of 100 prefabs were ready for occupation on the Eaves Green Road estate. Their completion had been delayed for some months by a shortage of concrete. At this time there was a waiting list of 1,100 families on the council's rehousing list. The Eaves Green Road council houses were also being built at this time, the first being occupied in April.

In July 1947, some 2,000 women were needed for work in local industry, 1,000 for cotton manufacturing and another 1,000 for clothing manufacturing. To help with this shortage, some 800 foreign workers, known as 'displaced persons', who were accommodated at Woodlands Hostel, were employed in these jobs.

The use of foreign workers was still a dominant feature of local industry for some time even into 1949, when two bus loads of Italian girls suddenly arrived in the town. They were also accommodated at Woodlands, where the Minister of Labour, Mr George Isaacs, visited them in November that year. A BBC recording unit interviewed the girls.

In 1948, road transport and railways were nationalised, and with the introduction of the National Health Service, Chorley and District Hospital was taken over by the NHS on 5 July. During the year, there were many electricity cuts, and it was reported in the local papers that '…the recent cuts by the Ministry of Fuel and Power seem to have been more frequent in Chorley than anywhere else. On top of which a large number of street gas lamps are not working. Many of the streets in the town only need a Hansom Cab, to imagine one is back in Victorian times.'

Another aspect of the fuel shortage saw many local families going out into the countryside to gather wood to use as fuel. Alas, in many instances the wood was obtained by cutting branches from trees, and even trespassing, which led to several cases being brought before local courts.

Surprisingly, even at the end of the 1940s there were still many restrictions on the purchase of goods. These were perhaps not as noticeable to us young people of the time, but to our parents the restrictions caused problems. This was especially so with clothing, for coupons were still being used for their purchase.

There was even a bit of snobbery about the clothes themselves. Remember the Utility Mark – label showing a symbol, that was affixed to clothing? It was a bit like a capital 'C' but thicker. Items of clothing bore one, two or even three of these symbols, for the system worked on the ratio of the more cloth in the garment, the more Utility Marks were needed. Of course, this was interpreted among children that the more Utility Marks on an item of clothing, the richer a child's parents.

The purchase of clothing, irrespective of the Utility Mark, was still used in conjunction with Clothing Coupons, and the higher the Utility Mark, the more coupons you had to use to purchase the item. I'm sure there will be some readers who will recall how, in the cloakrooms of Chorley schools, one tried to hide clothing with a low Utility Mark of perhaps just one symbol.

On 15 March 1949, the use of Clothing Coupons – which had been in use since 1941 – came to an end. The news was announced in a film 'short' by Harold Wilson, then head of the Board of Trade. Many shops in Chorley had sales the day after the announcement was made, and outside some shops – where notices stated 'Free from Coupons' – queues formed prior to opening.

The price of clothing at this time is reflected as follows: a man's two-piece suit, for example, cost between £9 and £12. And this was a memorable time for boys who had been overdue long trousers and were still wearing short ones. Now, with the coupon restrictions gone, they got their first long trousers.

Later in 1948, saw the first gas lamps in Chorley being removed, well in advance of the proposals to light some streets in the town with electricity. Some sources say that at this time the Big Lamp was removed from the end of Pall Mall. Others say that this rather special lamp, which should never have been lost, was removed later, in 1952.

Whatever the date of removal, the lamppost, which had begun life in the 1860s, with a single lamp on the top – it was later to have three lamps – was one of three which survived in Chorley until the early years of this century, the other two big lamps being in Market Place and the Cattle Market. The last survivor had affixed to it three signposts: to Coppull, Preston and Bolton.

The one that we remember was placed at the end of Pall Mall in the mid-19th century. It stood on a stone plinth and during the 19th century had a horse trough at its base. The main cast-iron post was very decorative and elegant, having a square base with floral patterned decoration. The square form altered to a round shape about four feet from the base. This part was tapered and fluted with gradually reducing diameters. The arms of the lamps themselves were later additions, yet were compatible in their design to the main post. Each of the three lamps had several mantles inside it.

Why the Big Lamp could not have been converted to electricity is a question which has been asked a large number of times since it was removed from its site. It was, after all, a part of Chorley's social history and as such could have been resited. We now have a replacement lamp, a replica, which seems to prove the point, that the public of Chorley were not happy about the removal of 'their' Big Lamp.

The lighting of the A6 trunk road became the responsibility of the Ministry of Transport in 1948, and by July 1949 the Ministry made the decision to improve Chorley's street lighting by announcing that Market Street would be lit with fluorescent lights, and that sodium lamps would be erected from Pall Mall to Yarrow Bridge, and from the Parish Church to the Sea View pub. The cost of this work would be about £9,570, of which Chorley Council was to raise half the amount.

In August, the Council decided that the new housing estate being built at the top of Harpers Lane, on Thornhill, would also be lit by electricity, using mercury vapour lamps. By the end of the year it was stated in the local Press that a third of the present gas street lighting in the town would be replaced with electricity, which would include another Big Lamp – no doubt a response to the many complaints from the public about its removal.

Work on the new A6 trunk road lighting was completed by October 1950, and at midnight on the 17th of the month, when there were very few people about, the lights were tested for the first time. The official switch-on, however, was performed by the Mayor after publicity ensured that the streets would be packed with townsfolk. As the crowds waited under the Victorian gas lighting, suddenly it was 'like daylight' again as the actinic fluorescent lights of Market Street and St Thomas's Road were lit amid cheers and a few comments to the effect that it was 'not before time either'.

'Electricity Fever' caught hold of the town when the public saw what a dramatic improvement the Market Street lights had made. Thus a decision was made by the Council (still known locally as the 'Corporation' at that time) to extend the street lighting quickly to the new Union Street, where property alongside the Parish Church had been demolished, to Cleveland Street, and along to Fazackerley Street before returning to Market Street. In addition, it was decided to extend sodium lighting to Wigan Lane and along Southport Road as well. The faces of the Town Hall clock were also lit for the first time.

It is interesting to take the local newspaper for, say, January 1949, and read the advertisements which tell us so much about life in Chorley at the dawn of the 1950s.

For instance, local mills were advertising for labour – at Talbot Spinning and Weaving, Cowling Spinning Co, Edge's Diamond Mill, Brindle's Greenfield Mill, North Street Mills, and Kem Mill at Whittle.

At Moore's of 90 Market Street, the following items of clothing were on sale: men's raglan overcoats, 39s 6d; men's blue melton overcoats, 59s 6d; a two-piece single-breasted suit, 89s 5d; men's cord trousers, 7s 11d; boy's cord lumberjackets, 18s 4d.

Meanwhile, at Mangnall's shoe shop in Market Street, ladies' shoes had been reduced from 50s 0d to 30s 0d. Perhaps someone had taken up this offer in time for the New Year's Eve Dance which had been held at Highways Hostel, with dancing to the Blue Stars Band.

At the end of the month, advertisements for dances in the town illustrated their popularity as well as showing just how many places there were to go dancing.

Dances for the coming week, as advertised on 28 January, included William Lawrence and Co's dance at St Mary's Hall, 7.30pm till 1.00am, at 2s 6d admission. Then there was the Chorley Co-op Education Committee's dance in the Co-op Hall in Steeley Lane. And the Victoria Dance Hall held dancing on Tuesdays, Wednesdays and Saturdays from 7.30pm to 10.45pm, admission 2s 0d. The Ambulance Hall staged a sequence dance, and St Mary's Hall was the venue for the CADOS annual ball. At the Tudor Ballroom, the 12th Lancs Battalion Home Guard Headquarters Company, Old Comrades' Association, were to have their annual dance.

Of the five cinemas to select from, one of them, the Plaza, used to stage live concerts on a Sunday evening. On Sunday, 30 January it was Teddy Foster and his Orchestra. The following Sunday it was Frank Weir and his Orchestra. The week after that it was the Radio Revellers in concert, advertised as 'Britain's No 1 Radio Sensation'. A hugely popular group at the time was the Ray Ellington Quartet, who were accompanied by the Billy Helm Orchestra when they played at the Plaza in early February.

Chorley's new Circular bus service was proving popular, according to the Press, and at Washington Hall, which had been turned into a Teachers' Training College, the second year intake of students took place. In April, a notice in the local paper explained 'How to get your New Ration Book'. It advised about the requisite number of forms to be filled in before you got your replacement book. Oh yes, you had to take your Identity Card along to exchange it at the local Ministry of Food office. At the end of April 1949, it was reported that 45,000 Ration Books had been issued, with some 3,000 or so still to be applied for.

Back to cinema advertisements, the following films were showing: *Meet the Huggets* at the Plaza; *Third Time Lucky* at the Odeon; *Sleep My Lovely* at the Pavilion; *Twilight on the Rio Grande*, with Gene Autry, at the Royal; and at the Empire there was *Keller McCoy*. Live on stage at the Plaza the following Sunday were Primo Scala and his Accordion Band.

Out of town, at Eccleston Rex cinema, three different films were shown during the week, the following were shown during the last week in April: *Her Sister's Secret* starring Nancy Colman; *Ginger*, 'the story of a boy and his dog'; and *Ghosts of Berkely Square* starring Robert Morley. The prices at the Rex were 7d, 1s 0d and 1s 6d.

The following week, at the beginning of May, Mr J. Tootell of Lighthurst Lane, Chorley, was home recovering from injuries sustained while serving in the Royal Navy. He was on board the destroyer *Consort* which was shelled while attempting to help release the Royal Naval frigate *Amethyst*, which had been trapped in China's Yangtse River. The Yangtse incident was certainly a memorable occasion and was later made into a film which was, of course, shown in Chorley, although it is not recorded if Mr Tootell went to relive his experiences.

The middle of 1949 saw Alderman Charlie Williams reporting to the Council that the bye laws of Astley Park were constantly being broken, and the riding of bicycles was regularly seen there. Some cyclists were subsequently fined for riding in the park. Fines were also imposed on cyclists for riding without lights.

At the end of June, holiday advertisements filled many column inches. Simms Coaches were advertising 'Cheshire Circulars' at 9s 0d, trips to Blackpool or Southport for 3s 9d and to Morecambe for 5s 9d. Cliff Owen's coach trips were priced at 11s 3d for Llangollen and Rhyl, 7s 0d for New Brighton, and a West Cumberland Tour for 14s 6d.

Turner's Coaches advertised a Derbyshire Peaks Tour for 9s 6d – the same price as to Harrogate and Knaresborough – and Gretna Green for 15s 9d. Tom Jackson's Coaches advertised 'quality coach travel', and Ribble Motors tours were priced at, £16 Ilfracombe and North Devon, all in for one week, and Bournemouth and the Isle of Wight, also for one week, at £16 10s 0d.

In July 1949, British Railways train trips from Chorley included half-days to Blackpool at 3s 6d, Bolton 1s 9d, Manchester 3s 3d, Leeds 7s 6d, and Morecambe 4s 3d. Full day excursions were offered to Carnforth 7s 4d, Grange 9s 2d, Ulverston 11s 3d, Barrow 13s 2d, and Windermere 12s 0d. That price of 12s 0d is 60p today, but when we consider that the wages of the time might be only £5-6 per week, then 12s 0d was a large percentage of that total.

In preparation for the holidays, the ladies hairdressers, Olettes in St Thomas's Road, offered full reconditioning treatment for hair at 35s 0d.

If you wanted to stay at home and not bother with a holiday, then you might want to spend the money you'd saved at Bullough's radio shop, where you could treat yourself to a 'five-valve all-wavelengths radio in an attractive cabinet' at £21 14s 0d, or 30s 0d deposit and 4s 0d weekly.

July was a month when some interesting events featured in the national Press. Remember the aeroplane which was described as the 'forerunner of the future', the very first jet-propelled passenger aircraft? This was the Comet airliner – and even that word seems old fashioned now. Its full title was the De Havilland Comet and its early appearance was made even more dramatic when, during taxing trials in full view of newspaper photographers on 27 July 1949, the test pilot said it felt 'right' to take off – and the plane did just that for the first time. Another first this month was the Bristol Brabazon aircraft trials. That is a name which might be remembered along with the Comet.

And how about the groundnuts affair? We knew them as peanuts, but officially, it seems, they were called groundnuts. This was a scheme which received a huge amount of publicity in national papers and on radio. It was introduced by the Labour Government's Overseas Food Corporation and operated in East Africa.

It involved the planting of large areas with groundnuts. The subsequent harvesting and processing of these would, allegedly, bring in a huge amount of revenue to Britain and East Africa, from the vegetable oil produced as the end product. We were told by Government ministers that the scheme couldn't fail, but it was revealed by the Tory Opposition that the cost of implementing planting and cultivation was far greater than the profits could ever be. This 'revelation' brought about the end of the infamous 'Ground Nut Scheme'.

What of local events in the latter half of 1949? Perhaps some readers will recall the Cross of Jerusalem that was being carried from Palestine and through Britain in August.

The cross and its carriers had rested in Bolton, and the next stage brought it through Chorley. It was met with crowds in Anderton, and a brief stop was made at St Joseph's Church there.

On arrival at Chorley, the carrier party was escorted through the town by a large crowd, to St Mary's Church where a special service was held, the church being filled to capacity. After a rest period and meal in the church hall, the carriers set off again with their 200lbs wooden cross, their route along Park Road being lined with people.

The cross was being carried across Europe and Britain by pilgrims to draw attention to the large number of religious sites in Palestine that were in need of increased protection to safeguard them for the future. The wooden cross, made in Jerusalem, incorporated pieces of rock from the site of the Crucifixion.

Back to prices. In August 1949, at Leslie's furniture shop, an oak bedroom suite cost £29, and an oak dining set £25, while £19 would buy you a Rexine three-piece suite, or for £12 you could purchase two fireside chairs.

Perhaps one of the least-known products made in Chorley since the mid-1930s, was aeroplanes! They flew from a field adjoining the Moor Road Works where they were made. The planes were built by the Moss Brothers who had a paint and varnish works in Crook Street, off Moor Road. The works survived until the 1980s and new housing now covers the site.

The planes, called Mosscraft, were built in four types, having radial engines. In 1949, in a fourth attempt, and flown by Mr W. H. Moss, one of the planes, which had been built in 1936 and had lain in storage at the works during the war and immediate post-war years, came fourth in the King's Cup Air Race. (The writer recalls seeing the plane whilst it was in store and covered in dust sheets.) The Air Race was broadcast on radio and was heard by many Chorley people.

At Astley Hall, restoration of the building began with work starting in the courtyard. Yet at nearby Astley Hall Farm, a serious fire in one of the fine stone barns, famous for its arched frontage, led to its subsequent demolition. At the end of August, an RAF Vampire jet plane, which had taken off from Samlesbury, crashed near Ellerbeck Colliery, Wigan Lane, and the pilot was killed.

Memories of the war, four years earlier, were still prevalent during mid-September when it was announced that households whose gardens contained Anderson air-raid shelters would soon see them removed. This caused concern in many households, where not only had the shelters become a place where memories had originated, but since the war they had also found further use as garden sheds. Also, many of the shelters now had flower beds over them, and to have them removed would cause many problems. It was later agreed by the Council that if the householder wanted to keep the shelter, they could pay £1 to retain them.

Towards the end of 1949, newspaper reports were discussing the jitterbugging and jive craze which had arrived in this country with the American servicemen who had been stationed here during the war.

It was also stated in the Press that the only rival to the dance hall was the cinema, although the new medium of television was being looked upon as a threat to that in the future. That was likely to be a long time away, however, because in 1949 only 25 per cent of the population of Britain could receive television pictures. Chorley received its first transmission towards the end of the year.

It is interesting to consider how television was envisaged to develop at the end of 1949. The film studio at Shepherds Bush had been purchased by the BBC for the production of television programmes. Many more transmitter masts would have to be built around the country to enable TV signals to be received by all. It was estimated that, by the end of 1950, enough masts would have been built to allow 75 per cent of the country to receive the signals.

In general, things were looking up after the war. There was plenty of work and more goods and services were available to people in many walks of life. Shops were selling labour-saving devices, and even fridges and washing machines were now available. And with the prospect of being able to watch a picture on a screen in your own home in the near future, life seemed very rosy indeed. Austerity Britain was slowly fading as the decade drew to a close.

This, then, was what life was like at the end of the 1940s. We were on the brink of a new decade, which was anticipated as being a period full of promise. With improvements in communications, we would be better informed about what was happening throughout the world, even if truly 'instant' news reporting was still not fully available until the advent of satellite broadcasting some 40 years later, when wars would unfold before our eyes as we ate our evening meal.

By the time the 1950s dawned, jet airliners had already made the world a 'smaller' place, at least for those who were lucky enough to afford holidays abroad. As yet the package holiday was a long time off. For most of us here in Chorley, holidays would still be in Blackpool, or at Butlin's Holiday Camp again.

For young people, the changes to come in education, travel, technology, even music and dancing, were beyond our comprehension. The world was rapidly changing and the 1950s would be our time to learn how we would fit in to this new decade, when we had left school. But it all seemed such a long way off...

WORLD EVENTS & CHORLEY MEMORIES

IT IS said that everyone can remember where they were when they heard the news that President Kennedy was assassinated, or when the Princess of Wales was killed, or even when England won the World Cup. Recalling major events can, indeed, often act as a trigger to more mundane memories.

It might be, then, that the reader can recall other events which took place in Chorley, due to associating them with national and international events. These wider events certainly helped me to remember local happenings, in addition to my own diaries and jottings from the time. It may well be that my contemporaries of the period will also be prompted into recalling what we were all doing in and around Chorley during the period of the later 1940s to the 1960s.

Where exactly to start with this story is difficult, for I write from a very personal point of view, of what I knew and was involved in. We all recall certain periods of our history, be they local or national events, and, after all, history is all around us.

Those who were born from the mid-1930s to the mid-1940s, and who were to grow up through the 1940s, 1950s, and 1960s, will recall the events of that time with comparative ease. Yet to those born since that time, the period being discussed is as much a part of past history as is the life of Henry VIII.

Despite the war only coming to an end in 1945, the threat of another world war was still very real in those post-war years. At first the theory was that it would erupt in the Middle East, sparked by the conflict between the fledgling Israeli nation and its Arab neighbours before engulfing the world again.

The atomic bomb was another talking point. Its use to bring the war to an end in Japan, by dropping it on Hiroshima and Nagasaki, was still a recent and vivid memory in our minds. Now the question was what would happen when other nations and alliances obtained nuclear weapons, as they inevitably would.

In 1950, the Korean War began. Like many conflicts before, it was regarded as a war that would soon be over, but this was not to be. Korea had been divided into two countries in 1949. The North was controlled by the communist regime, who, on 25 June 1950, invaded the non-communist South in an attempt to unite the country under communism. Immediately, the United Nations called on its members to send troops, and 17 nations did so, the largest contingent coming from the USA. Many British soldiers also fought in that inhospitable terrain and there was much gallantry and at least one VC was won in Korea.

UN forces counter-attacked and drove the communist forces back to the North, actually forcing them beyond the original border and further to the north. This caused China to send in its own forces in support of the North Koreans. The communist forces drove the United Nations back to the border, and for a time the battle moved back and forth across that border, the 49th parallel. This went on until 1953, when a peace accord was finally signed.

The Home Guard, disbanded at the end of the war, was partially reformed in 1950, at a time when world affairs seemed to suggest that a prolonged peace was not yet something we could look forward to. Locally, at the Royal Ordnance Factory (ROF), Chorley, there was also a switch back to its primary function. The workforce had been reduced from some 25,000 in the war years to 5,000 or so. Production of ammunition had ceased and the factory turned over to peacetime work.

A clothing factory was set up inside the ROF, and two plants were installed for the production, of concrete railway sleepers. These were in great demand due to the lack of wood imports during the war years.

Another big shortage in the post-war years was housing and here, too, the ROF played a vital role in the manufacture of prefabricated sections for Airey Houses which could be assembled within two weeks by non-skilled men. Several of these houses were built in the Chorley area, for example in Charnock Richard, Euxton and Hoghton.

The workforce at ROF Chorley had been further reduced to below 4,000 but then the factory started producing ammunition once again and needed more labour. In August 1950, the workforce stood at 4,400, and would increase moreso.

Does anyone recall Red Petrol, as used in 1950, and the tax increase on petrol as well? This took the price of a gallon of petrol up to 4s 2d from 2s 1d. Due to this increase, all local bus fares went up within a year, so that in early 1951 the prices on most journeys increased by a ha'penny or even a penny.

July and August 1950 saw changes around Chorley town centre which were aimed at improving traffic flow, although it was very much a matter of opinion as to whether or not these trials were a complete success. First, the new improved Union Street was opened to traffic, closer to the Parish Church than old Union Street had been. But the traffic flow was one-way only, towards the bus station.

Fazackerley Street was made one-way, towards Market Street, the traffic passing through it having to turn to the north. The lower end of Chapel Street was also made one-way, traffic using this having to turn south in Market Street. Two other streets made one-way at the same time were Back Mount and Mealhouse Lane.

So far as local industry was concerned, during 1950-51 the shortage of women in local mills gave cause for concern because many of the foreign workers, who lived at the hostels, had moved to other parts of Britain or emigrated altogether. By August 1951, local mills were particularly short of young persons for all types of work within the cotton manufacturing trade. The Heapey Works of Thomas Witter and Co, which had been a bleachworks until destroyed by fire in 1944, was rebuilt and had started manufacturing chipboard and a lightweight floor covering, like oilcloth, which was printed with bright coloured patterns and called 'Balatum'. This was cut to size at Fosterfield Mill and Lower Healey Works.

During 1951, improvements to road safety in Market Street took the form of railings being fitted at the edge of the footpath between Mount Pleasant and St Thomas's Road on one side, and from the bottom of Chapel Street to High Street on the other. It was hoped this would do more to prevent accidents. The railings replaced a series of single metal posts which had extended most of the way as mentioned above, but had only chains stretching between them. This allowed the public to duck underneath them and cross Market Street wherever they wanted. Not only was this dangerous to themselves, but was extremely hazardous to drivers as well.

Incidentally, prices and makes of cars being advertised in the local Press during 1951 were, for example: 1933 Standard 9, £150; 1933 Standard 3, £120; 1937 Standard 12, £35; 1936 Austin 7, £30; 1938 Morris 14, £60; 1934 Hillman 10, £30. New cars, for example, were: Austin A30, £360 plus £131 7s 0d tax; Ford Prefect, £395 plus £165 14s 2d tax.

Perhaps one of the most enduring memories of the early 1950s, in particular 1952, was the illness and subsequent death of King George VI, on 6 February. He was aged 56. He had come to the throne following the abdication of his brother Edward VIII. King George VI was buried on 16 February 1952.

Another February event was the abolition of Identity Cards on the 21st of the month. Five days later, Prime Minister Sir Winston Churchill announced that Britain had now developed her own atomic bomb. In October, Britain exploded her first nuclear bomb. In May, the jet airliner, the Comet, began its first commercial flights.

At the end of September, I was visiting relatives near Wembley, during which time I walked around the Harrow area, taking in the school and other attractions. During that walk, being keen on railways, I visited the station at Harrow and Wealdstone, had a look around, and continued over a footbridge on my walk.

One week later, the second worst rail disaster in Britain occurred at that very station. On 8 October 1952, 112 people died in a three-train crash. It happened when a Perth-London express ran into a local commuter train which was stopped in the station. Almost immediately, another express, having left Euston a short time before, en route to the north, crashed into the wreckage of the other two trains. A further 200 persons were injured in the accident. The carriages of the trains were piled 50 feet high and destroyed the footbridge I had so recently walked over.

It still remains a very evocative memory due to my visit there, but there was another factor which was disconcerting for railway enthusiasts of the time. One of the expresses involved had been pulled by the recently-converted Turbomotive, which was now a conventional steam locomotive called *Princess Anne*. Its conversion had only taken place a short time before the accident. The locomotive was too damaged to be repaired, and was scrapped.

On Friday, 22 February 1952, a bad accident took place in one of Chorley's mills. It happened as the mill was closing down for the weekend.

The machinery in the mill, on each of the floors, was driven by line-shafts which ran the full length of the mill. Along the lineshafts were driving pulleys which had belts driving the cotton machinery. The lineshafts were driven by ropes from the main engine flywheel, to the ends of the lineshafts.

To stop the mill engine, it was first necessary to gradually stop the lineshafts on each of the mill floors. As the line shafting was gradually slowed down, so too was the main engine speed, by the controlling steam 'governor', thus bringing the engine to a stop. This was the normal way that things were done.

But, in this instance, it seems that the machinery on each floor of the mill was stopped too quickly, without consideration being given to the slowing down of the main engine driving the mill. As the engine governor was unable to cope with such a sudden slowing down, the inertial weight of the flywheel caused the engine to speed up, to such a speed as to cause the disintegration of the flywheel itself.

Large pieces of this 25ft-diameter cast-iron flywheel were flung around the engine house at great speed, some of them passing through the roof, and flying some 200 yards to penetrate the roofs of houses in Trafalgar Street, between Park Road and Water Street. The accident caused one death and a serious injury. It was indeed amazing that there were no other fatalities.

1952 was also the year when Chorley Charity Carnival raised funds for Chorley Hospital, the Darby and Joan Club, and Weldband Prize Band. The procession had a large number of floats, was of a substantial length and included many floats from industries outside Chorley. The carnival started on the Flat Iron, its route being Clifford Street, Water Street, Harpers Lane, Eaves Lane, Brook Street, Lyons Lane, Duke Street, Pall Mall, Moor Road, finishing up on All Saints' field behind the school, where the Carnival Queen, Anne Todd from Adlington, was crowned by Miss Hibbert.

Newspapers of the early 1950s were telling us about the advantages of owning a car. But to most people this was out of the question. In the north, it was the coach that was the way to travel on excursions into the countryside or to the coast. In fact they all seemed to come through Chorley at the weekend, or so it seemed when you tried to cross Market Street.

In 1952 it was reported in the national Press that on the roads of Britain were 2,762,000 cars. These were driving around with a minimum number of traffic lights, road signs, and roundabouts on the roads. The most common way of traffic control, especially in the town, was by policemen on point duty.

In view of the excess traffic passing through Chorley during weekends throughout the 1950s, policemen on point duty were usually at least three in number. It was a time when more Belisha crossings were being requested by the public. Police point duty locations were usually between Queen's Road end, and the Park Gates, mid-Market Street, and at the Duke Street-Lyons Lane crossroads.

It was this crossroads which was a favourite place for many of our fathers and grandfathers at that time. This was often the place to where the traffic backed up at the weekend, all the way from the Town Hall. Here the traffic watchers would while away the time, watching the vehicles passing, and commenting on their types and size etc. No doubt there would also be comment about the driving skills of some drivers, although most of the watchers could not drive anyway.

Another reason for this being a much favoured place to stand and watch the passing traffic was that there were several hostelries which provided a drink if it were needed. At the end of Standish Street was the King's Arms, and across the road, the Wagon and Horses at the end of Leigh Street.

At the end of Lyons Lane was the Borough, while a little way along Lyons Lane was the Green Man Still. Between the end of Duke Street and the Plaza was the Princess Royal. At the other side of the Plaza, were the Eagle and the Duke of York. Across the road again, at the end of Queen Street East, was the White Bear. It is not really surprising the men all liked to go 'up Duke', to 'traffic watch'.

Of course, the area referred to as 'up Duke' was the crossroads of Bolton Street and Bolton Road, with Duke Street and Lyons Lane. It was a busy junction, more so at weekends. It was a place where accidents often occurred, hence the watchers. This busy crossroads first saw traffic lights installed, on trial at first, during 1959 and permanently during early 1960.

Today, following the creation of the town bypass and new traffic flow system, it is hard to recall what the area was like then. Yet, this part of the town termed 'up Duke' was as well-known as 'near Big Lamp' which meant an area at the end of Pall Mall.

Of course, as well as cars and coaches, lots of commercial wagons used Chorley's roads because many local firms had their own vehicles. There were the two laundries of Briggs and Hygienic, both of which had their own vans. And the local mills took delivery of raw cotton from Liverpool Docks and beams of warp thread from other mills throughout the county.

During 1948 came nationalisation, when we saw the creation of British Road Services. Many boys of the time, including some in Chorley, took up 'wagon spotting'. The boys watched for BRS wagons, obtaining their depots and registration numbers. It was something different to do I suppose, and it made a change from train spotting.

These wagons were a lot different to those of today with many of them, like the local buses, manufactured by Leyland Motors. There was the very smart new bus which came out in the 1950s, produced by Leyland, the Royal Tiger with its white paint and new styling. It was used on the express runs when it first came into service.

This was about the same time as the new double-decker bus came out, these also being mainly white in colour and referred to as the 'White Ladies'. These, too, were used on express work initially. Both these new types of bus were 'state of the art' then, and rather up-market. To travel on them was greatly different to the buses we had been used to.

Of course, the canals were still being commercially used then. The Leeds-Liverpool, running through Chorley's east valley, carried cargoes of raw cotton to the mills built on the canal sides. Others would bring coal from Lancashire's coal mines.

Often the canal boats, en route to or from Liverpool or Leeds, would tie up in Chorley. Some favoured spots were at Heath Charnock, Froom Street, or Botany Bay. Chorley's mills had raw material or coal brought by canal in the 1950s included Cowling New Mill, Cowling Bridge, Redan and Gilletts at Cowling, then Barkhouse Mill, Talbot Mill and beyond Botany railway viaduct, Canal Mill.

In the early 1950s, canal boats were often still pulled by horse and this transportation was used for a rather special event by many Chorley organisations, especially those with church affiliations who hired them for Sunday School trips.

We would enjoy the annual outing by canal boat, leaving from Froom Street or Botany. From our starting place, we would be taken perhaps to Red Rock at Haigh, where we would have a great time exploring and generally playing, then have a picnic tea before returning to Chorley again. Simple pleasures I suppose, but enjoyable enough.

Britain's role as a world power had declined by the early 1950s, at least from what it had been in the early years of the 20th century. The country was, after all, still counting the cost of the war. The Empire was still virtually intact, although the Hindu lands of India had become self-governing in 1947, while the northern parts of the sub-Continent, the Muslim areas, became East and West Pakistan.

Still at school as we were, however, politics were a long way from our thoughts, although we were being told in 1950, the year of a General Election, that it was a time of rebuilding and one of finding our way again. Also that the 'young people of today' would greatly benefit from the setting up of the Welfare State. Although the Labour Government was re-elected, their second victory since the war, we, as young people didn't really know what this so-called Welfare State was all about, nor did we really care.

Still dominating the international situation, of course, was the nuclear age. The bomb, we were being told, would become a deterrent. Atomic energy would be used as a new source of power, to produce electricity for instance. There were many, of course, who said that the awesome power of atomic energy would never be a safe power source. There was also the point that research into atomic energy was being carried out in many countries, some of which were not friendly with the west. The Cold War was upon us and there were many potential flashpoints.

During the early 1950s, the Middle East was under particularly close scrutiny from countries whose ships used the Suez Canal. Britain's involvement with the Canal had begun in 1875 when she bought the majority shareholding in the Canal Company which had been held by the Egyptian Government since 1869, following the completion of the vital waterway by the French.

The Suez Canal was made an International Zone, the Canal Zone, and was guarded by British troops under an agreement with Egypt. In June 1956, following unsuccessful negotiations with the Egyptians relating to these duties, British troops were withdrawn. A month later, following a request from the Egyptians for the British to help finance the building of a new dam at Aswan, which was refused, President Nasser of Egypt nationalised the Canal.

Britain and France began negotiations to try to restore the Canal Zone again, but at this time there were problems along the Egyptian-Israeli border, giving rise to much concern. Escalation of border incidents continued through mid-1956, and in October of that year, Israel invaded Egypt.

With the intervention of many Middle East countries, the fighting eased, with Israel standing down. But Egypt did not and was thus seen as the aggressor. British and French forces invaded Egypt but the United States strongly disapproved and the fighting ceased almost immediately after paratroopers had been dropped. The forces were eventually replaced by a NATO peacekeeping force in the Canal Zone.

The Suez Crisis, as it became known, was seen as a great humiliation in that it demonstrated that in affairs of international importance, Britain's ability to act on her own was much reduced.

During the crisis the Suez Canal was closed to shipping in both directions and on a personal note, I was serving as Engineer Officer on the P & O passenger liner *Strathmore*.

Our passage back to England was to have been from Freemantle in Western Australia, to Colombo (in Ceylon – as it was then), then Bombay in India, and from here across to Aden, then via the Red Sea to the Suez Canal for transit into the Mediterranean. We arrived in Bombay without any hold-up, but were informed by the company that we were to proceed from Bombay to Durban, South Africa. From there we went via Cape Town, northwards to England.

Not only was the time of the voyage greatly increased, but so too was the mileage travelled on our return from Australia to England. This came to a total of 17,410 miles steamed and took 51 days. There was another aspect of the voyage home that was significant in that we had to cross the Equator three times during the course of the voyage, as opposed to the normal, once only crossing from the Southern to the Northern Hemisphere.

Events in the Middle East in the early to mid-1950s overshadowed other things that were happening in the world and at home. For example, the Soviet Union's premier, Joseph Stalin, died in 1953; in Kenya, Yomo Kenyata was eventually jailed for his involvement with the Mau Mau regime; and in Yugoslavia, Marshall Tito became president.

The North Atlantic Treaty Organisation, formed in 1949 with great hopes and aspirations, received much newspaper coverage in the early 1950s and there was a UN Secretary-General, with a hard name to pronounce, one Trygve Lie. He was replaced in 1953 by another with an equally difficult name, Dag Hammarskjöld.

In 1954, the island of Cyprus was the scene of several serious disturbances between the Cypriot Government and Greece, relating to the division of the island.

To avert the spread of communism in South East Asia, the South East Asia Treaty Organisation (SEATO), was formed. Another pact, in 1955, was one within Eastern Europe. This was the Warsaw Pact and was a treaty drawn up between the Eastern European countries under communist governments, to safeguard their borders against western intervention. It was, indeed, the direct 'opponent' of NATO.

Continuing with 1955 events, the situation in Cyprus got progressively worse and escalated into terrorist activities under EOKA, the Greek Cypriot group. West Germany, meanwhile, was admitted to NATO, while in Argentina, an armed rebellion forced President Peron into exile. But what was happening in England, and more especially in Chorley, during this period?

One of the more memorable events of the early 1950s was the death of King George VI in February 1952. I particularly remember the radio broadcasts of the time and how, with such sad voices, announcers would report on the King's illness, and how he was becoming worse, although his death was a shock to everyone, not least his daughter, the new Queen Elizabeth, who was in Kenya on an official visit. The death of the King came after another General Election in 1951, when a Conservative Government was elected.

An item which I bought in the 1950s is still one of my prized possessions – a five shilling piece, or a crown, which was specially minted for the big event of 1951, the Festival of Britain. This was held in London, alongside the River Thames. I was fortunate enough to be able to go down to see this very special exhibition about all that was great in Britain, and what the future had in store for the country. It was certainly a revelation to me and left many memories.

Perhaps one of the lasting impressions was of the buildings erected for the Festival, for their architectural styling was something new. Indeed, one of the Festival's themes was how things might look in the future. Some of the exhibitions were in buildings which had names such as the Dome of Discovery or the Skylon. The latter was apparently unsupported, a tall pencil-like erection, held in place by thin wires.

Today there is nothing left of the site except for the Royal Festival Hall. The Festival of Britain advocated a much brighter future for the country as a whole, a welcome thing in the so-called age of austerity which was supposedly now coming to an end, although some forms of rationing were still with us, even so long after the end of the war.

Newspaper headlines about the Festival of Britain might have been saying, 'It was a tonic for the country,' or that it was filled with 'fantasy, fun and colour', but, as our parents were saying, things were still not completely back to normal. Mind you, if, like me, you were still at school, or had just left, then all these things really didn't mean a lot.

In Britain, in 1953, we were all anticipating the forthcoming Coronation of Queen Elizabeth II. This was the first major event where the full pageantry of such an occasion would be shown to the entire nation at the same time – if you had a television set that was, and only then if you were able to receive a good picture signal. Potentially, the whole nation would have been able to see the event, with the above provisos, but as it was, it was not seen live by a very large audience. But where it was seen on the television set – actually it was called a 'receiver' then – crowds of people watched tiny little screens in friends' and relations' houses, or stood in front of shop windows in the street, to see this wonder of live pictures coming from London. We had to wait to see its full splendour in colour at the local pictures, though.

I recall watching that first transmission, with its flickering black and white image, and wondering, as we all did, if it really would catch on. Of course, radio was still the main communications medium – not just the news broadcasts, but for all the shows that were on as well. I suppose parental association with the radio was another thing which made us, the teenagers of the time, listen to the programmes. After all, we had grown up with radio too.

The Coronation saw events the like of which had not been witnessed since the end of the war – street parties up and down the length and breadth of Britain. They took place during the week of the Coronation, some before, some after, but most on the day itself, 2 June 1953.

Chorley, of course, had its street parties like the rest of the country but not too many them seem to have been photographed, or at least the photographs haven't been unearthed.

Many of those who did take photographs of Coronation street parties would probably have done so using the old Kodak Brownie camera, a 'box' camera which had perhaps not been used since before the war. This was certainly the case so far as my own parents were concerned and their camera, a Brownie, was usually to be found at the bottom of the wardrobe. It would be a long time before the sophistication of today's cameras was introduced.

When you went to the chemist's shop for a camera film in those days, the size of film you asked for would be like using a foreign language today. You asked for a '120' or a '620' film. Only professionals used 35 millimetre film. As we have already noted, most ordinary people used the 'box' camera.

And to paraphrase what Henry Ford was alleged to have said about motor cars, when it came to film you could have any colour you wanted, so long as it was black. Colour film was another thing which as yet was not generally used – the complete reverse of the 1960s to 90s when everything was done in colour by machine printing, and it cost a small fortune to have black and white film processed.

The pageantry of the Coronation overshadowed other events which took place in the first half of 1953. There were the severe storms which occurred in January that year, when the coastal areas of eastern England and Scotland, together with the north coasts of Belgium and Holland, took great seas blown by north-easterly winds. Huge amounts of damage was done to all these coastal areas, and on the continent large areas were flooded.

On 20 January, General Dwight D. Eisenhower was inaugurated as the 34th President of the USA, but March 1953 saw a sad event in Britain with the death of Queen Mary. She was much revered and lived to be 85 years of age. I always remember Queen Mary as being very tall and very much the royal matriarch. She was, of course, the widow of King George V. Another famous person who died in March this year was Joseph Stalin, the Russian leader. In April, Winston Churchill was made a Knight of the Garter.

On Coronation Day, the headlines in the national newspapers ran something along the lines of 'The Crowning Glory'. They were not referring to that day's forthcoming events, however, but to the news that New Zealander Edmund Hilary and Sherpa Tensing had become the first men to reach the summit of Mount Everest.

The Coronation retained people's interest for some weeks afterwards, with cinemas showing the first colour footage of the great occasion and magazines also featuring it heavily.

Elsewhere, though, other significant events were under way. The British steel industry was denationalised and on the other side of the world, in Korea, an armistice was signed in Panmunjom.

One of the more menacing events that took place, was the reported detonation of Russia's first hydrogen bomb. The use of nuclear weapons as a deterrent to aggression took on a new turn now that all the major powers seem to be so armed and with such weapons being pointed at each other.

In Britain in September, capital punishment was being debated in Parliament and a Royal Commission recommended that juries should recommend whether or not the death sentence or life imprisonment should be given to those they found guilty of murder. It also recommended that the laws which applied to those accused who claimed insanity should be amended.

On a brighter note another aspect of the rationing era came to an end, with the abolition of sugar rationing, which had been in place for 14 years.

Towards the end of the month, Professor Auguste Piccard dived to a depth of 10,000 feet in the Mediterranean off the coast of Italy to set a world record.

Sir Winston Churchill was in the news yet again during October when he was awarded the Nobel Prize for Literature. And a great archaeological discovery, made some years earlier, was found to be a hoax. This was the skull of the so-called Piltdown Man, believed to have been the earliest human remains found in Britain. As techniques for dating bones, fossils and other ancient artifacts had improved over the years since the original discovery, so it was established that the skull was in fact a hoax, albeit an elaborate one which had fooled the academics of the archeological world since 1911 when it was allegedly found in a gravel pit, together with flint tools which made it even more convincing. Finally to the last month of 1953 and to a December that was the mildest for 20 years.

The post-war years saw a gradual improvement in employment levels, despite the associated problems – such as obtaining components or raw materials – which had dogged companies starting up again after the war. Such was the case in Lancashire, where raw cotton imports were a problem in the immediate post-war years. Also, some cotton mills were not allowed to open unless sanctioned by central government.

Additionally, many mills and other factories which had been shut down for the duration of the war now had problems starting up due to their equipment being in poor condition. Other works, meanwhile, had been engaged on war work and now had to re-equip before resuming their peacetime operation. And demobilisation meant that the armed services were pouring manpower back on to the civilian job market, although this was done slowly to avoid a huge number of men and women suddenly being placed on the unemployment registers.

Locally, of course, we have already referred to the thousands of employees at the Royal Ordnance Factory at Chorley suddenly becoming surplus to requirements. Fortunately, many of these did not live locally and the unemployment figures in Chorley were not excessively high.

Regardless of the immediate post-war years and their problems, however, Britain had begun to prosper in the very late 1940s and early 1950s and most people were in work and had a little more money to spend once the industrial problems had been overcome.

Returning to the general events of the early to mid-1950s, television was making greater inroads, helped no doubt by the televising of the Coronation, and in 1956 it was reporting graphic accounts of events in Eastern Europe. The Soviet Union invaded

Hungary, following an uprising by the Hungarian government and its people against harsh Russian policies. East Germany, too, was in turmoil, and so far as Britain was concerned, the Suez Crisis had been a humiliation which seemed to hasten the end of the British Empire.

In 1957, Prime Minister Anthony Eden, whose health and reputation had deteriorated in the aftermath of Suez, was replaced by Harold Macmillan and within two years of his becoming Prime Minister, Ceylon, Ghana and Malaysia had become independent while there were plans in the pipeline to allow nations in the West Indies and Central Africa to become independent. The Empire was dwindling and eventually would disappear, the overwhelming majority of the countries which had made it up becoming self-governing and equal members of the British Commonwealth. Eventually, that organisation would drop its 'British' tag.

Britain might have become a member of the European Economic Community in 1958. Eventually they joined in the 1970s, but the original concept of a purely trade organisation was being abandoned in favour of political union into a 'United States of Europe'. Certainly the 'Common Market' of the 1950s was a long way from what became the reality as a new millennium dawned.

In the home in the 1950s, the American way of life was making inroads and very soon central heating would become the normal thing to have in your house (although air conditioning is just as far away as ever it was). Television sets, washing machines and refrigerators were also available.

Even so, during the 1950s, wringers, as they were called, instead of the old fashioned squeezers, were still available in the shops, as also were dolly tubs and possers. And a large number of Chorley households still had to do their weekly wash in the kitchen or separate washhouse in the back yard, when hot water was provided by making a fire under the clothes boiler. When the boiling was completed, the washing process was continued by putting the clothes into the dolly tub and agitating them with the wooden, or copper bottomed, posser.

But that was not the end of the process, for after washing and rinsing, the excess water was removed from the clothing, by passing them between wooden rollers, which were turned by a large handle. The process, of turning the squeezers, or mangle, was often the job of the children of the house, as I am sure many will recall.

So far as central heating was concerned, that was something that was not commonplace in the late 1940s and the 1950s. Most of my closest friends of that period lived in and around Queen's Road and Southport Road and into Windsor Road in Chorley. Of all these, perhaps ten or twelve houses in total, only two had some sort of central heating, which was similar to the old systems we used to have in schools, with big radiators.

Of course, it was the 'stiff upper lip' factor that delayed the mass installation of central heating – that and the cost. Many people just shrugged and said that they'd got along fine without it so far, so why did they need it now? Stepping on to cold linoleum and having to scrape ice off the inside of the bedroom window was never my favourite way of getting up on a winter's morning, although the ice made interesting patterns on the glass.

As yet there were no supermarkets, but there was still a pawnbroker's business in Chorley through the 1950s. This was Messrs Dennerley's which was originally on old Union Street brow, alongside the Parish Church, until it was demolished about 1951. The shop relocated to the bottom of Byron Street, on the corner with Union Street. Many readers will remember the splendid decorations in the shop window for the Queen's Coronation in 1953. Perhaps there are some people in the town today who can recall their parents having to use the services of this, the last pawnshop in the town.

I spoke about having an aunt and uncle in Clifford Street. He was a favourite uncle who told tales of his army days in Africa, and who had a splendid tinted photograph of himself wearing a white uniform and tropical helmet with feathers on it. In Chorley, he knew a huge number of people, probably because he worked for the Council on dustbin collection. He was a collector of horse brasses, and visited farms in the area with me in tow, as he wheeled and dealed.

His horse brasses were much sought after when the Americans were at Washington Hall Camp, and due to them always calling on him, I was never short of chewing gum, and I also visited the camp for parties. The Americans left Washington Hall at the end of the war, so the story is perhaps just within the mid-1940s.

My uncle's interest in horses and their paraphernalia took him (and me) to blacksmiths in the town, such as at the corner of Livesey Street and Clifford Street, where the large shire horses were shod. I knew this smithy quite well and vividly recall how I used to cry when the hot shoe was being fitted to the horse's hoof, producing smoke and an acrid smell. I used to think the horse was being hurt.

Most of the big shire horses were stabled off Cunliffe Street, and opposite to the Pavilion cinema in Salisbury Street. Here, a building was owned by Messrs Nall and Company, haulage contractors. They used horses only, and worked from Chorley Railway Goods Yard delivering goods in and around the town.

In the 1950s, hire purchase, or 'HP', was popular with some, and nicknamed the 'never-never' by many. Once again there was the typical British reaction – "We're not buying anything unless we can pay for it," – and because of this, on a principle, a large number of households did without items they needed. Of course, it did prove popular with others and many shops began their own schemes, using a payment book. Even if you didn't want anything at the time, you could put a few shillings a week away, until you did.

There was a move towards having a cleaner atmosphere and we started to hear terms such as 'smokeless fuel'. Through various mediums, we were introduced to 'Mr Therm' of the Gas Board, who was associated with economy. But the majority of houses in the country still used coal fires, which created a mixture of smoke and fog which was called 'smog'. This was so bad in the big cities, especially in London, that visibility was down to a few yards and it affected people's health. Today, smog is just a memory and many houses don't even have chimneys, for central heating is commonplace now.

Another aspect of those coal fire days and the periods of smog was that of the contribution that may have been made by steam trains, so much a part of the 1950s, and indeed for most of the 1960s as well. As I went to Blackpool often, with parents and my friends from Chorley, it was invariably by train. And always leaning out of the window of the train, trying to see other steam locomotives, my eyes would stream with tears or finish up with a piece of coal ash in them. The carriages would have separate compartments and there were no corridors on most trains, especially those on local services. It was a bit upmarket if you were on a train which had corridors so that you could move around and have access to toilets.

In the later 1950s, my friends and I became adventurous and travelled to Butlins at Pwllheli. These were perhaps what could be called the 'formative years' of our lives …learning how to stay awake all night, playing cards and then missing breakfast because we'd had very little sleep.

Of course, road and rail transport took a lot longer then, and it might take all day to reach some holiday destinations once you'd decided that Blackpool wasn't far enough away. It would be about 1954 when one of my Chorley acquaintances announced that he was going abroad with his parents. Abroad! This was truly an adventure then, and a rarity as well. Jumping on a plane at your local airport for a fortnight in the sun wasn't even dreamed about.

It's odd how some things come into the mind when recalling a bygone era, take the fire engine for example. In the 1950s, when they dashed to a fire in Chorley, there was no wailing siren – just a firemen ringing a bell! Chorley's fire station was originally located in Back Street across the road from Albion Street. Back Street was behind St George's School at the end of Pall Mall, or the Big Lamp area. It has gone now, having disappeared when the Pall Mall Triangle was cleared away to create a huge 'white elephant' building on the site of the former school.

Indeed, this so-called triangle at the end of Pall Mall saw a lot of the town's older places of interest cleared away. Apart from the fire station there was the public abattoir, which had cattle pens and hay lofts accessed by ladders cut into flat planks affixed to the walls.

Perhaps one poignant memory which will be recalled by many, is that it was to a chamber (operated by a council department) in the fire station yard that family pets were brought to be put to sleep if they were old or too ill.

There was, however, another important feature in Back Street, at least so far as the male population of the time was concerned. Close to the end of Back Street, on the footpath close to Bolton Street, was a public urinal. This was not your common stone-built public toilet – it was made from plates of cast iron with holes and slits near the top for decoration, and must have dated back to Victorian times. Shades of Clochemerle, in Chorley? A similar cast-iron urinal is still to be seen alongside the Parish Church at Ormskirk.

Then there was the public toilet in Chorley which was a traffic hazard! This was on Park Road, almost opposite the gates to Astley Park. During the 1950s, when traffic queued through Chorley in both directions, coach drivers had time to see where public toilets were located. On the return journey, coaches stopped opposite the park gates for passengers to use the nearby facilities – and it was that which caused an obstruction to other traffic.

These relatively small irritations aside, however, the new Elizabethan age seemed to create a mood of optimism throughout the land. After all, life was becoming easier and the population more prosperous. There was a greater awareness of what was happening in the world and at home, and an increased interest as well, partially aided by the new medium of television.

Even the world of sport seemed to give an impetus to the general public endorsing what today we would call 'the feel good factor'. In 1953, Stanley Matthews helped Blackpool win a famous FA Cup Final. Indeed, it was forever to be known as the 'Matthews Final' although it was another Stanley – Mortensen – who had scored a hat-trick in the glorious fight-back over ten-men Bolton Wanderers. What price an FA Cup Final being contested between these two Lancashire club's today?

The elusive sub-four-minute mile, which had been a 'Holy Grail' for middle-distance runners, was eventually achieved by a British athlete, Roger Bannister, in 1954. It all helped to make people 'feel good' about being British – the so-called 'feel good factor'.

Before moving on to 1954 in detail, there are a few points relative to 1953 which I feel deserve to be noted. They are perhaps personal, yet applicable to many households at the time of the Coronation. They are associated with external house decorations. It was a time when we were proud to be able to display the Union flag. We did not need planning permission to do so, nor was there any move towards hanging the flag of St George as a replacement for the Union flag.

One of the problems about hanging the flag from a bedroom window was firstly how to secure the pole so that it remained straight, and how to stop the flag wrapping itself around the pole in the wind. The first problem was overcome by dad securing a mophead bracket to the window frame, into which the flagpole was inserted. To keep the flag hanging downwards, little bags of sand were sewn to the lower edge.

At this time we were living in Farrington Street, where the Courthouse now stands. In the 1950s, there were houses each side of the street. All these had flags hanging from their upstairs windows, and also had various coats-of-arms, made from wood fastened to the front walls. But this was not all, for bunting was hung from house to house across the street, along the whole of its length, like it was in many others.

Farrington Street had some interesting properties adjoining it, some of them being quite an age. The street ran from Crown Street, at the west end, and was named after Crown Mill, a former cotton mill which later became Sumners Corn Mill on St Thomas's Road. On St Thomas's Road-Crown Street corner, was the house of the police superintendent with offices which extended to the entrance gateway to the police station yard, At the other side of the gates to the yard, were the offices of the local weights and measures officers.

At the Crown Street-Farrington Street corner, the buildings surrounding the police station yard were used as garages for cars and motorcycles. These ran down Farrington Street to adjoin three police houses, which were separated from our house by a narrow passageway. Despite the rebuilding, that passage still exists today, between the court building and the police station.

On the same side as the courthouse stands today, and roughly in the same place, was a large workshop used as a joiner's and coffin maker's workshop. This stood next door but one to the house I lived in. During the 1940s it was run by a man called Lucas, whose house was on the corner of Farrington Street and Crown Street. Today it is used as the Chorley Blind Welfare Centre.

This house had the best gable end in the street, and was often used by the children who lived nearby as a place to bounce footballs or smaller balls from. But we were often told to 'clear off' due to the sound of the balls hitting the wall being heard inside the house. As Mr Lucas and my father were friends, I was often tasked with helping out in the workshop, being given such jobs as sweeping up, heating wood glue, cleaning the gas engine etc. For misbehaving, I was often put into unfinished coffins, and the lid put on… only for a few moments that is.

One of the interesting aspects about this workshop was that buildings to the rear adjoined other backs to those properties on Town Hall Square. The significance of these buildings, which were standing until demolition in the early 1960s, was that parts of them still had stables and loose boxes, with hay mangers and lofts over. Whether these were part of the farms which stood around Town Green, or were later stables and coach houses, is unknown, as no recording of them was carried out, when the area was demolished.

Another point about this end of the street, which was unadopted, was that it led to Back Mount (old maps of this part of the town refer to this section of the street being called Skittle Alley), which itself contained interesting buildings, one such being the Red Lion Tap, a very small pub which adjoined the Red Lion pub across a courtyard.

Horses and coaches were stabled in this courtyard, for the Red Lion, like the former Gillibrand Arms which stood on the site where the Town Hall clock tower now stands, was a coaching inn. The Red Lion stood in Mealhouse Lane, where the courtyard entrance also was. Following demolition, the Red Lion was replaced by the White Hart.

It is only with hindsight, that we realise how much old property there was in Chorley in the 1940s to 1960s. Some of these properties were very old, certainly of early 19th-century origins, some possibly older than that, and all of them a part of the town's social history.

These old properties were located in Bolton Street, Bolton Road and streets off them. They were in terraced rows, many having cellars which were formerly used for handloom weaving. Similar housing could be seen in Market Street, Anderton Street, Alfred's Court, Fleet Street, Cheapside and in Pall Mall. Here, adjoining the Eagle and Child, was a courtyard with very old tenements around it. Very little of the old property in these areas is still visible today.

Elsewhere in the town, these old handloom weavers' cottages could be seen in Chapel Street and Eaves Lane-Harpers Lane corner. Further along Pall Mall, at the junction with Tootal Street, were more old cottages with others forming Black Horse Street. And on Moor Road, almost opposite All Saints' Church, was Chorley Colliery Yard with miners' cottages fronting Moor Road itself.

Major redevelopment of the old property within the town started during the later 1950s, when work began on clearing the Bolton Road and adjoining streets of its old, and by now, unfit property. This clearance continued into the 1960s with new council house estates being built to accommodate those in need of rehousing.

Meanwhile, despite World War Two having finished only a matter of ten years earlier (basing 1955 as our nominal date) not only were things in Chorley changing with the removal of old property, but so too was the world itself, and another 'war' had revealed itself. This was the so-called Cold War, which had arisen between the two great powers of the world, the USA and USSR. This had escalated into an East and West divide, the communist regime in the East and the capitalist system in the West.

Mention of 1955 brings to mind the event that took place in the Town Hall that year. Did any readers contribute to the Hobbies Exhibition which was organised by Chorley Rotary Club in September? The exhibition brought together over 20 local clubs and organisations, who had stands to display their particular hobby or interest.

It was the sort of thing which, if revived on an annual basis, would be of as much interest to the public as it was in 1955. At that exhibition, the townsfolk of Chorley were surprised by the diversity of clubs catering for so many interests or hobbies. It would be the same today, if the Hobbies Exhibition became an annual event.

To bring this section of our look at world events and Chorley memories to an end, let us recall a few more events that took place as the 1950s drew to a close and the 1960s dawned. We'll start with 1958, a year when, in Chorley, the annual Holiday Weeks saw good weather, Chorley being almost like a ghost town as so many people had gone away by train or bus.

Early 1958 will be recalled not just by football fans, but by everyone in Manchester generally and even elsewhere. On 6 February, an aircraft carrying the Manchester United football team back from a European Cup match crashed during take off at Munich. Seven of the team were killed outright and an eighth, Duncan Edwards, died later. Journalists and other passengers were also killed and many of those who survived were badly injured, including the manager Matt Busby. The whole country reeled under the news and, in many, ways, the tragedy gave birth to the mystique which has surrounded the club worldwide ever since.

In December 1958, the first motorway in Britain, the Preston bypass, was opened. Two months earlier, the Cod War between Britain and Iceland had flared up. The first STD phones were introduced and the Hovercraft made its maiden voyage or 'flight'. In 1960, Francis Chichester won the first single-handed transatlantic yacht race, and National Service came to an end in December that year.

MORE CHORLEY MEMORIES

Chorley Boys' Club

AFTER the war years, the youth of the country struggled to come to terms with the return of normal family life. It was something which had been almost forgotten by children born before and during the war. Families had been split up with the need to evacuate children from towns and cities likely to be bombed. And, of course, many fathers and brothers had been away for years and returned as virtual strangers.

Much of the adult male population – and a large number of women – were in the services, while women not in uniform filled the role of the absent men in factories etc. For instance, a huge number of women worked in the Royal Ordnance Factories, producing munitions. With all these upheavals, which varied throughout the country, it was hardly surprising that getting back to normal was difficult.

From the later 1940s, almost to the mid-1950s, central government and local authorities were aware of the need to nurture young people who had suffered the trauma of family upheaval in the war years. This, of course, was particularly so in cities like London, Liverpool, Manchester, Coventry and Hull, which were subjected to the Blitz and therefore the need to evacuate their children.

Irrespective of personal circumstances, the youth of the time were catered for by many organisations and people who were concerned with their future. One of the schemes set up was the Duke of Edinburgh Awards, to give impetus to the need for youth to be catered for in all areas such as education, sport, leadership, pursuits and religion.

Young people were encouraged to join clubs or organisations such as the Boy Scouts, Girl Guides, Boys' Brigade, service cadet forces and youth clubs, all of which were suited to both sexes. In 1953, Chorley saw the formation of a Boys' Club. The founder and secretary of this was a Mr Hurst.

This first club was set up in a house in Brown Street, opposite the end of Bowland Avenue. This was the former home of Mr Brown, the owner of the adjacent four-storey cotton mill. Later, this mill was used by Messrs Chortex Ltd, being referred to as Chortex Mill.

During the next four years, the old detached house was subject to conversion, starting with the ground and first floor. Eventually it was necessary to open up other rooms and to extend and modernise the building to create the best environment for the Boys' Club.

One of the main sports which was promoted by the club was boxing and at least two of the Chorley Club boys made a name for themselves, and the town, by winning titles. One of these was Brian Collinson, who became a National Boys' Club champion in 1957. Appropriately, this marked the official opening of the club.

The official opening, four years after the founding of the club, was performed by the Duke of Gloucester in the presence of local dignitaries and Superintendent Cook of Chorley Police Station, who was a great supporter of the Boys' Club movement.

From its foundation, the club had no problems in attracting members and it soon became very popular, and at times was often full to capacity. It filled a great demand for boxing and its supporters enjoyed bouts with other clubs both in and out of Lancashire.

In 1958 the club saw another champion. This was Harold True, who became amateur heavyweight champion of East Lancashire and East Cheshire. The club continued in popularity into the 1960s, a drastic event taking place in June 1963 when a fire completely gutted the building.

Despite its loss of equipment, the club continued to function on a temporary basis wherever it could find accommodation. In the meantime, the committee and supporters investigated ways and means of raising money to rebuild the club. It was eventually the County Council who provided the money for a club on a new site, at the end of Lord Street, off Steeley Lane.

In addition to the Boys' Club becoming established in Chorley during the 1950s, the Army Cadet Force was formed, plus the St George's Pipe Band who played before the Queen in July 1958. That was also the year that the Chorley Round Table's first Charity Carnival took place. The youth of the town were encouraged to take part and the guest of honour on the carnival stage was comedian Ken Dodd.

Yet in some ways the concerted efforts to put young people on the 'right path' created an air of rebelliousness among the youth of the 1950s. It was as if they resented being 'organised' and wanted to do 'their own thing'.

It was also the era of the Teddy Boys and rock 'n roll music. Our parents began to ask, 'Where will it all end?'

Housing in Chorley

THE 1951 Census Return for Chorley showed that the Borough had a population of 32,640. Plans for new houses in the town had been mooted in the immediate post-war years, but house building materials were in short supply. As a stop-gap, prefabricated houses were decided upon, the first of these being built in Hodder Avenue off Eaves Green Road.

The specific areas proposed for new major house building were on the north side of Moor Road, off Tootell Street and Liptrott Road, plus the enlarging of the extant estate to the south side of Moor Road, extending to Weldbank Lane. This was Eaves Green Road, an area which was used for building council property in 1945-46. Similarly, additional property was to be built in Brown Street, on the Highfield Estate which had seen its first phase completed in 1947.

On another new council estate, known as Thornhill, 60 houses were under construction during 1948, the houses being designed by a well-known architect of the time, Mr Frank Bradley. Work on the new housing estate of Tootell Street, in 1946, saw the road system being laid out. (Readers may recall the old footpath to Walletts Wood with railway sleepers each side of it. That path disappeared about this time but had started about where Coniston House now stands.)

A familiar complaint from many people on the Council waiting lists was that the houses were not being built fast enough. By January 1952, work on the Tootell Street estate was being carried out over a 30-acre site, with 114 houses and bungalows being occupied. It was envisaged at this time that one year hence, in 1953, some 1,000 people would be living on the estate.

In 1952, private house building was under way again and about 50 per cent of the house licences granted to the Council by the Ministry of Local Housing and Government was for private housing. At this time, January 1952, there was 600 names on the Council house waiting list. Most of them could not afford the deposit for private houses, which varied between £150 to £200.

A large number of the private houses, were built in the Duxbury-Yarrow Bridge area to the south, and to the north beyond Hartwood, up to the farm adjoining the concrete water tower which supplied the necessary head pressure for drinking water to the town's supply. (The water tower was demolished during 1998, after being redundant for some time.)

During the next two years, the Council house waiting list had been reduced as more new houses were built. With this increase, the need for an improved sewage scheme for Chorley became necessary. A plan for this work to be carried out, in the East Valley off Eaves Lane, was costed at £150,000. Unfortunately, 1956 saw a reduction in government funding to local councils for schemes such as the one intended, and the work was set aside for the time being. In fact when the work was eventually completed in the early 1960s, the original cost had gone up by £300,000, to a total of almost half a million pounds.

In discussing the housing situation in Chorley through the 1950s, it is necessary to refer back to the 1940s. Many of the housing schemes which started during the 1950s were only completed during the 1960s. Indeed, some of them were only completed too far into the 1960s, to qualify for inclusion in this book.

Of course, Chorley had a lot of old property which had become unfit for habitation. However, many of those living in them objected to the Council sanitary inspector's decision. But the Council's guidelines of 1954, appertaining to the condition of such property and the lack of amenities etc, placed them in the slum category, which meant that they became subject to a demolition order.

In late 1954, some 400 houses in Chorley were unfit and would have to be demolished. This figure was constantly under review. Many potential new householders were having to vacate their old houses in advance of demolition. Despite their homes being declared unfit, most of the residents did not want to leave the houses, or streets, in which they had lived all of their lives and where they knew all the other families living there.

The review continued over the next two years and in late 1956 the latest review stated that the number of 400 houses to be cleared in 1954 was now nearer to 1,000. Demolition of the condemned property started in 1956. The first area cleared was around the Botany Bay district. Here, a large number of 19th-century properties had been built for the men and women working the barges on the canal, or at Botany Bay itself.

Botany was, during the late 1700s and through the 19th century, the port for Chorley and was a busy community, remote from Chorley itself, almost like a rural village. One of the streets there, called Long Row, ran parallel to the canal, from Botany Bridge towards Bagganley Lane, and was renowned for its fighting, and its beerhouses, together with the very poor condition of the property itself.

The Botany community, even in 1851, was still like a separate township, having its own blacksmith, clogger, muslin manufacturer, two pubs, mordant manufacture, grocer's shop, wheelwrights and tailors, besides the work associated with the loading and unloading of canal boats.

Along with Long Row, other property in Botany was cleared from Blackburn Road adjacent to Botany Bridge. The old canal warehouse, built in the 19th century, was the very last of the old property to be cleared, and that was only when the motorway was built in the 1970s, which necessitated a new bridge being built over the canal at Botany Bay. That bridge crosses directly over the site of the old warehouse.

In view of the great changes which have taken place relating to the use of the canal today, it is unfortunate, I believe, that an old building such as this warehouse was cleared away when it could have formed an attractive canalside feature for Botany Bay. During the 1950s the warehouse was used only as a store for canal maintenance.

Looking at the area around Botany today, it is hard to imagine how it was 60 years ago. To picture that scene, one has to stand on the old canal bridge and look over the stone parapets. Looking to the north, the Leeds-Liverpool Canal disappears into the centre distance, and on the left, the M61 motorway runs parallel to it. Between them is the Botany Bay Village complex, created in what was Messrs Widdows Canal Mill, a former cotton mill.

Between the old canal bridge and the mill was a stone railway viaduct of eight arches with embankments either end, carrying the railway high above the canal. This was the Wigan-Blackburn (via Chorley) line. The viaduct was demolished in the late 1960s, allowing the motorway to be built. Close by, the Railway pub is a reminder of that former railway.

At the other side of the old bridge, looking to the south, can be seen the actual Botany Bay, once described as Chorley's port. Here, canal boats were loaded and unloaded, using the old warehouse described above. Again the canal runs away to the south, but the view is obscured with the new Botany Bridge as well as, in the distance, another bridge over the canal carrying the motorway itself.

In the 1950s, though, this view was very different. We kids looked over the bridge parapet to see canal boats moored in the canal basin, and a stone warehouse on the left-hand side. In the distance, we looked down the east valley, with a background of Healey Nab, and could see the chimney, water tower and upper storey, of Talbot Mill.

Moving to the other end of the town, to Bolton Street/Road area, here too, major demolition works were begun. This area was occupied by a large number of old stone cottages with cellars, These properties were used for handloom weaving during the early 19th century, and were generally in a poor state of repair.

These cottages were in Albion Street, Standish Street, King Street and Queen Street East. as well as along the east side of Bolton Street and Bolton Road. By 1957, most of these old cottages were well on the way to becoming memories only. Today, for instance, it is hard to realise that the forecourt of Chorley Ford when in Bolton Street, used to have a row of these old cottages standing between Standish Street and Burlington Street.

Also hereabouts, at the bottom of Standish Street, used to be a pub called the King's Arms which, in recent years, became Messrs Rimmer's car dealers. Next door, in Standish Street itself, was the Model Lodging House, often called, Standish Street Lodging House.

This was another of the buildings in Chorley which catered for the down and outs of the time, in the days when we used to see tramps passing through the town. They would stay at the lodging houses overnight or for longer periods, depending on the time of year. It was said that one type of overnight stay at the Common Lodging House in King Street consisted of sleeping on a rope, whilst standing up and actually leaning on the rope. At least this ensured they had a roof over their heads for the night!

The word 'tramp' is something else which has gone from everyday usage, like the lodging houses they used in Chorley. Today they would be called vagrants. Some of them used to come and go through Chorley on a regular basis, almost seasonally.

I recall from schooldays how we would talk to some of them, perhaps sitting on the wall around the Parish Churchyard, or on the market stalls. They told us stories of where they had been since last in the town, sleeping rough most of the time, yet they never really seemed to complain about their lot.

There was one man who lived at one of the lodging houses who worked in the gardens around the Queen's Road, Southport Road and Windsor Road area, who spoke very correctly, without a regional accent. He seemed to have come from a good background and fallen on hard times. He once told us how he worked in many large gardens of the gentry and moved around from 'bothy to bothy'. Everyone knew him as Percy.

I only wish, in retrospect that I had taken notes during some of the tales from those men of the road. Another of the men once told us that he had walked from Land's End to John O'Groats, over a period of years.

Returning to housing in Chorley we must refer to the 1970s when the Central Lancashire Development Corporation (CLDC), was set up. It was intended to create a new town based around Chorley, Leyland and Preston. There were many objections to these plans to reshape our rural areas, and the compulsory purchase of so much good farmland.

In fact, this was a scheme which was some 25 years old. In 1947 it was mooted by central government that Manchester's overspill population would be settled in the Central Lancashire area. One of the problems with this proposal was that there was a waiting list for houses in Chorley for local people, who complained that these 'overspill' people might be getting priority treatment over local families.

There were still squatters in Chorley during the 1950s, at Lower Healey Works at the bottom of Froom Street. A former bleachworks, during the war, it was an army detention camp or 'glasshouse'. It was the army huts which were used by the squatter families, who were still there in 1957.

To return to the Manchester overspill population, the mid-1950s had seen a shift in the thinking for the centre for this new town. It was now to be based around Eccleston, with Leyland and Chorley at the north and south ends respectively. By 1958, there was another shift in the proposals, this time leaving Eccleston out of the plan and utilising Chorley and Leyland only.

It also emerged in the later 1950s that the alternative location for Manchester's overspill population was Lymm in Cheshire. When this was divulged, there was quite a lot of gossip that Lymm was a bit 'upmarket' so we in the Chorley area would get the overspill people.

The numbers of houses to be built for the new town were being estimated at 17,000, with large concentrations in Euxton, at Runshaw, and off the A6 road at Whittle where there was space to build. Most of the areas envisaged for development have been utilised since, under the CLDC's 1970s outline plan, although they built on the land mainly during the 1980s and 1990s, they continue even now in 2012.

The 1950s was also a time when new industries were desperately needed in the Chorley area. This was just another of the problems, on top of land availability, to be presented to the County Council. There were also the squatters desperately needing proper housing, and the demolition, clearance and rebuilding programme for the houses in Chorley itself, such as on those on the Council estates. In 1959, a situation became apparent in that more jobs needed to be created for persons without houses – the people who wanted the houses had no money, for they had no job!

So far as the 1950s new town proposals were concerned, it was in 1965 when the Preston area was designated to be the centre of Lancashire's new town to encompass Bamber Bridge, Leyland and Chorley. These new proposals once again caused objections and public inquiries throughout the whole of the designated area.

By the early 1960s, the estates of Thornhill, Tootall Street and Highfield were either completed or very nearly so. In Bolton Street and Road, the clearance of the old properties and the rebuilding with Council bungalows and flats was mostly finished. The older Council properties were given facelifts at this time, in Ashby Street and off Harpers Lane in the Beaconsfield-Shakespeare Terrace areas.

More private houses were being built during the late 1950s and early 1960s. Many of these were built on land where old properties had stood, having been within areas earmarked for clearance. There were many of these smaller areas around the town which were cleared during the 1950s and upon which private building was carried out after demolition.

One of these small areas was alongside the Eagle and Child pub in Pall Mall, where a grassed area can be seen today. Yet, in the 1950s there was a narrow entrance to a courtyard surrounded by old properties. At the top of Cannon Street and Alfred's Court off Market Street stood old property. In Fleet Street and Moor Street were more old stone 19th-century cottages, all of which were cleared away by the early 1960s. But it was already under consideration that the estates already built would not be big enough and that more sites for council property would be needed.

Entertainment and Television in Chorley

LIKE many parts of the country, Chorley looked upon the coming of television with a sense of detachment. Everything seemed to happen in London first and the statement that this wonderful new medium would soon be available to everyone in the country was viewed with some cynicism by the citizens of a northern industrial town in the early 1950s.

Yet during 1951-52, the coming of television loomed larger and larger. TV receivers started to appear in dealers' shop windows in the town, with advertisements advising: 'Get ready for Television coming to Chorley'. Some adverts used the town motto: 'Be Aware of Television Coming.' Even the Boy Scouts' motto 'Be Prepared' was used in some advertising campaigns.

The first flickering television pictures I saw were in one of the electrical dealers in Market Street. This was called Stewart Porter's and occupied the shop which today is next but one to the Trustee Savings Bank. That was in early 1953, when test transmissions were being carried out.

The spread of television throughout the country is part of our social history, and initially, the coming of the system was not seen as being in any way 'anti-social'. In Chorley, like so many other towns throughout the country, the decline of the cinema as a result of television being available to everyone was not fully envisaged.

As I have said before in this book, during the 1950s Chorley had five cinemas, Indeed, until 1946 there were six in the town.

Today, two buildings which housed cinemas – Odeon and Empire – remain. Sadly the art deco Plaza was finally demolished in December 2011. Films are still shown by Chorley Film Society in the former Empire Cinema (Chorley Little Theatre).

In the 1950s they were magical places where we could escape from reality for a couple of hours or so. Some had the same film running all week, which was actually six days because in the early part of the decade there were no Sunday cinemas. Some Chorley cinemas changed their programme twice in the week.

Films were shown in Chorley from about 1909 up to 1986, starting at the Public Hall in Mealhouse Lane and ending with films at the former Plaza, later to become Studio Two, then ultimately Studio Four,

It is interesting to consider generally the role of the various cinemas in Chorley's history. The Public Hall, where the first films were shown before World War One, stood next to the Red Lion in Mealhouse Lane. The rear exit from this building was next door to the Red Lion Tap in Back Mount and the building was used for meetings and social events well before the first silent movies were shown there with piano accompaniment. The building later became the Chorley British Legion.

The Pavilion, off Cunliffe Street, was originally built as a barracks for the Chorley Volunteer Rifles during the late 19th century. During the 1920s it was converted into a cinema, where its rear double seats were popular. It closed as a cinema in 1962 and became a bingo hall. After a few years in this role, it was converted back to a cinema in 1972. But only five months after re-opening it closed once again, this time, for good.

Chorley Hippodrome in Gillibrand Street was built as a theatre in 1909, although the theatrical productions were interspersed with films from soon after the building was constructed. During the 1930s and through the 1940s, the Hippodrome was used more as a cinema than as a venue for live theatre. In 1946, however, it became a theatre once again and apparently Bill Waddington, the actor who played the *Coronation Street* television character of Percy Sugden, was one who played on the stage here. In 1947, conversion of the cinema began, after which it emerged as the Tudor Ballroom.

In 1967, while under Coral Leisure Group, the Tudor Bingo Club as it had become, was sold to be converted into a supermarket, having the name Graham's. Under this management, the former stage was removed in January 1989 to allow further extensions to be carried out in the store. The supermarket closed in 1997. Planning applications for alterations to the building were made in late 1998, demolition work beginning in February 1999. The site is still undeveloped in 2012.

The Royal, built in 1911, was another theatre. It was considered that its stage was almost as high as its auditorium. with dressing rooms at the sides and underneath. It had a balcony and, above that, a gallery which was more popularly known as the 'Monkey Rack'. Under the auditorium, was the billiard hall accessed from steps in Market Street.

The Royal began showing films in the 1920s, becoming the Royal Cinema. In the 1930s, when refurbishment was carried out, the Royal was renamed the Royal Super Cinema. It retained its cast-iron and glass canopy in front of the building until late in its cinema days, in the 1940s.

The Royal stood empty during most of the 1950s, being used for only occasional functions, some of which were piano playing 'marathons'. One of these during the mid-1950s starred 'Musical Marie' from Bolton, who played all day and all night to set a new record of some kind. I recall how we tried to catch her out during the evenings. Even during the night, we would go into the Royal to see if she was still playing. She always was.

In 1959, the former theatre was purchased by Whelan's, a Liverpool company who demolished it and built on the site Chorley's first supermarket. This was a relatively early such store to open, for the idea of the so-called supermarket had only been introduced into the London area during 1957.

Eventually Whelan's sold to Lennon's and it continued as a supermarket. Lennon's was eventually bought by the Gateway supermarket chain. Yet strangely, Gateway were not there for very long, the store closing after only a few months. Finally, the building was altered yet again to become one of the ubiquitous McDonalds hamburger restaurants. Mc Donalds relocated and the building has been disused since then.

Around 1922, the Empire became the first purpose-built cinema in Chorley. Its claim to fame, however, came in the 1950s when the film *Rock Around the Clock* was shown. This had been banned in many towns throughout the county, but despite this the Empire went ahead, risking 'over enthusiasm' by followers of the music played in the film by Bill Haley and his Comets. Many local authorities apparently viewed Rock 'n Roll as decadent!

Of course, there was no trouble among the young people watching the film, many of them having come from neighbouring towns.

The Empire cinema was among the first in the county to show widescreen films and yet another first for the Empire, over the other Chorley cinemas, was the showing of 3D films, where you had to watch wearing cardboard spectacles, one lens being red, the other green. We all ducked as objects were thrown toward us, knives and arrows appearing to come right out of the screen.

The Plaza opened in March 1937 and as this was the Coronation year of King George VI and Queen Elizabeth, there was some consideration that the name should be the Coronation Cinema. Despite being built primarily as a cinema, the Plaza had dressing rooms for live shows to be held in the spacious modern building. There was also a small restaurant and an upstairs lounge.

By 1941, with the growing popularity of the cinema organ, one such organ was installed here, and throughout the war and afterwards, live Sunday night concerts became popular at the Plaza, as discussed in more detail elsewhere in this book. Names to have appeared included Joe Loss and Jack Hilton, and Chorley's own Joyce Gartside, who sang songs from *Madame Butterfly*.

Chorley's Odeon cinema, the last to be built in the town, was opened in February 1938, having plush upstairs and downstairs foyers, and Art Deco plasterwork in the auditorium. Its flat-topped roof was used by fire watchers during the war. Through the 1950s it was regarded, like the Plaza, as being one of the 'posh' cinemas where one went on Saturday nights. The Odeon closed in 1971, and is used today as a bingo hall.

Despite there being five cinemas in Chorley during the 1950s, again as we have mentioned elsewhere, another very popular pastime among young and old was dancing. Here, too, the town had a large number of dance halls, Yet even in a new millennium, neither cinema nor dancing are well catered for in Chorley, ironically in an age when we are all supposed to have more leisure time.

In 1953, the Town Hall Assembly Room reopened for dancing after being utilised by the local Food Control Office for some time. Several church clubs had dancing at weekends, St Mary's Hall in Devonshire Road and the Parish Church Institute perhaps being the best remembered venues.

There were also working mens' clubs and the Co-op Hall. This was in Little Steeley Lane, where the first Chorley Co-op shop was opened, becoming the headquarters of the local movement. Then there was the rather 'up-market' dance venue of the Royal Oak, where many of the town's official functions took place.

Additionally, there was the Ambulance Hall in Fleet Street, and close by in Gillibrand Street the former cinema and theatre, the Hippodrome, which as we have already seen, was converted to the Tudor Ballroom. In Duke Street was Leyland Motors Club, while for younger people, a much favoured dance venue was the Vic where we had an interval pass-out stamped on our wrist. It was the place which catered for the 'emerging' teenager, playing their kind of music in less formal circumstances than most dance halls of the area.

But there was another place which started up in the 1950s and which catered for the younger element. In fact it was the first place in the town to serve the needs of teenagers only. It was in Botany, in Knowley Brow, and was called the Hot Spot, which became Chorley's first disco.

And, of course, in addition to the dances themselves there were also dancing lessons. These, too, were held in the Vic – or to give it its proper title, the Victoria Dance Hall – over the Victoria Arcade. Ballroom dancing was also taught off Eaves Lane in Colyton Road.

Just out of town there was Highways Hostel which had a wonderful sprung floor and its own orchestra. There was also the Euxton Institute and the same at Eccleston, which had its own cinema, the Rex, as did Coppull, Adlington, Croston and Brinscall. At Rivington, dances were regularly held at The Barn, while in Euxton Lane, the ROF Club was a popular venue at weekends.

Of course, all these pursuits – cinemas and dancing – were under growing threat from television. The signal for the first television receivers in Chorley had to come from some distance away and was not too clear because the first local transmitting mast, on Winter Hill, had not yet been built. But sales in Chorley were given a boost by the purchase of several receivers by Chorley hospitals.

Of course, the fact that a TV image could be seen at all – and could transmit events as they happened – was of enormous benefit to sales, despite the poor image. As we have already discussed, for those lucky enough to have access to a television set the Coronation of 1953 had been seen in Chorley as it happened, but for the rest, the earliest opportunity to see the events in London came a week or so later when they were shown at the cinemas.

With special offers from local shops, the early inducement to purchase a TV receiver led to many households in Chorley buying sets in readiness for the much better pictures which we were promised would be available in the not-too-distant future. There were even instances where people purchased only the aerial, which they then attached to their chimney. This, of course, was the early 'X' shaped aerial as can be seen in many photographs. Indeed, by the mid-1950s, most of the streets in the town sported a TV aerial on one or two, or even as many as five or six houses. But at the other end of the aerial wire, there might not actually be a television receiver.

In 1955, with television gathering support but with others fearing that cinemas would be adversely affected, it was decided that a poll should be held in Chorley to decide whether or not cinemas should be allowed to open on Sunday evenings.

In November that year, arguments for and against were put to a packed Town Hall Assembly Room and the result was 4,708 being for the motion and 2,106 against. A month or so later, final approval was given by the local authorities.

The next stage in Chorley's evolution into the era of television was when a TV programme was broadcast from the town. This came about following the building of the Winter Hill transmitting station in 1956, which ensured better quality pictures would be received by most of Chorley's townsfolk, although some surrounding villages would have to await the coming of booster transmitters before they received good quality pictures.

This first television broadcast from Chorley, in 1957, was of a boxing tournament between Chorley Boys' Club and other northern and London-based clubs in the Town Hall. The transmitting of the programme from the Town Hall to Winter Hill, led to the erection of a temporary dish on the Town Hall roof.

Between 1956 and 1959, reports of the rivalry between the mediums of television and cinema were rarely out of local newspapers. During the late 1950s, a *Brains Trust* was televised in Chorley, again from the Town Hall, the questionmaster being the well-known McDonald Hobley, and one of the panelists being Chris Chataway, the Olympic athlete who later went into politics.

In 1959, General Election year, television was first used by candidates to put forward their manifestos, but the TV presentations were blamed for poor attendances at meetings in Chorley, where the prospective candidate talked directly to a live audience.

Chorley's Labour candidate, Clifford Kenyon, appeared on television, on a programme called *Election Marathon*. The main point for debate was nationalisation, a topic which provoked a great deal of discussion from both audience and panel.

But not many Chorley people saw these programmes being transmitted from their own town, despite the argument that television was keeping the public away from meetings. There was simply not yet television in everyone's house, far from it, although perhaps 40 per cent of houses per street now had aerials on their roofs.

During the late 1950s, it was not yet considered to be anti-social to watch television. Indeed, there was a gradual increase in the numbers of friends visiting the homes of others who had a television receiver. It was still being called the 'miracle of the age', to see live pictures coming into your home.

The cinemas had begun to realise that to survive as they had done so far, would be difficult in the face such competition. They would have to change in some way, if they were still to attract people from the comfort of their homes.

Another entertainment in Chorley beginning to feel the pinch was amateur dramatics. Not only did the town have a general group, the Chorley Amateur Dramatic and Operatic Society or CADOS, but some churches also had their own groups of players. These stage productions were generally well received by the public, who preferred to attend live shows locally rather than travel to places like Preston and Bolton.

But in the 1950s, CADOS began to see a reduction in audience attendances. In 1952, CADOS had resumed at their former St George's Street venue, below the Baptist Chapel, which had been used during the war years as a café, CADOS having had to re-locate to Highways Hostel, which also had an amateur dramatics group.

Many people put the decline in attendances down to television, but it was contended by some that the fall off was due more to their re-location, where it was necessary to carry out structural alterations which the group did not have the money to carry out. Because of this problem, the group moved again, this time to the Ambulance Hall in Fleet Street.

The late 1940s and early 1950s had seen an increase in demand by the general public to see more live shows on the stages of their local communities. The scope for amateur dramatics was very wide, from murder mysteries to musicals.

During April 1953, at St Mary's Hall in Devonshire Road, Chorley, a stage production of *The Mikado* was performed to full-house audiences throughout the week of its showing. It was the first time that *The Mikado* had been performed in the town for 18 years.

Press reports said: 'The revival was due to the longstanding absence of the show, especially after the war years. Now, a new generation has grown up without seeing such shows, and hearing the music associated with it. They have grown up being cradled in war, and nurtured on Jazz and Bebop.'

In 1955, the television broadcasting monopoly enjoyed by the BBC came to an end. On 22 September, for London viewers initially, the first commercial television channel began operations. For the first time advertisements were shown on television, the very first extolling the virtues of Gibbs Toothpaste.

For those who were not yet receiving television in the home, radio was still the main source of entertainment with a wide range of programmes. Apart from variety shows like *Blackpool Night*, there was *The Archers* serial, which had followed on from *Dick Barton Special Agent* with his friends Snowy and Jock.

We were glued to the radio at quarter to seven on weekday evenings to find out what would happen to Dick Barton. The signature tune, *Devil's Gallop*, always evokes memories of those times when everything came to a stop to listen to the radio for that precious 15 minutes.

Returning to *The Archers*, I must confess that I became a regular listener. On the night when the first commercial television programme was being transmitted to London viewers, in Chorley, as in many other places in the country, we were more than ever glued to the radio and *The Archers*. For on this night, the stables at Brookfield Farm burned down and Grace Archer died trying to rescue here beloved horse, Midnight.

An interesting occurrence took place at the Empire in May 1957, when strange voices could be heard which were not part of the film, a Western called *Texas Rose*. There was much speculation as to where these faint voices were coming from, ideas which ranged from hauntings to police cars.

In fact, the latter theory was almost correct because the voices were coming from new police radio sets which were introduced during this year and used on VHF frequency. As the Empire was the only cinema to pick up the signals, and as it was the nearest cinema to the police station (it ceased showing films in December 1957) the mystery was soon solved.

With the Empire closed, the building was put up for sale and interest shown by local businesses, one of these proposing to turn the premises into a garage. During the first half of 1958, the former cinema was up for sale. In August and September it was leased, and in the event altered internally to become a wrestling venue.

Wrestling was a sport which had become very popular in the late 1950s, due to it being shown on television. The Empire continued to provide wrestling entertainment until 1959, when attendances started to fall. Once again, the building was put up for sale and the possibility of it being turned into a garage loomed once more.

The former cinema, Chorley's first purpose-built one at that, was also noted by the CADOS supporters who desperately needed a place to call their own, having had to relocate to different venues in the town.

Initially the asking price for the building was too much for an amateur organisation to afford, but eventually this difficulty was overcome and the purchase of the building by the Chorley Amateur Dramatic and Operatic Society went ahead. They moved in, returned the former cinema seating and created the Little Theatre. This is still the venue of CADOS, in the new millennium.

The increasing march of television in the home gathered momentum during the early 1960s, with better transmitting facilities – the new booster stations had been built in the outlying areas. Television sets increased in size and became commercially more available.

On the chimneys of many houses in the Chorley area, evidence grew of the popularity of television; now the streets had perhaps a 70 per cent figure of homes sporting a television aerial, all of them now actually connected to a television 'set' as they were now known. This figure increased all the time and television was now influencing the 'teenager', which was now a term in everyday use.

In 1959, 'Teenage Culture' had fully emerged, TV programmes such as *Oh Boy!* promoting their kind of music. Some of the popular singers of 1959-60 were Bill Haley and the Comets, Guy Mitchell, Johnnie Ray, Frankie Laine, Tommy Steele, Elvis Presley, Jerry Lee Lewis, Michael Holliday, The Everly Brothers, Connie Francis, Craig Douglas, Cliff Richard, Adam Faith, Johnny Kidd, Roy Orbison, to name a few only, who made it to the top of the hit charts.

In cinemas, the effect of television was now being noticed in Chorley and elsewhere. Saturday night cinema queues were now a thing of the past. Television was top of the popularity poll. It was the new age of entertainment, when you could stay in your home to watch brand new variety shows, plays and comedy series

This, then, was entertainment in Chorley in the 1950s. It was still a time when you went with parents to visit aunts and uncles at the weekends, to play cards, or one of the games which has now either got a new name, or passed into history, such as Lotto, Crown and Anchor, Put and Take. But all that was swiftly changing too.

In the following pages, are some 300 photographs which should evoke a few memories, and stimulate some conversation about *Chorley Through The 1950s*.

MARKET STREET TO BOLTON ROAD

This aerial view of Chorley town centre was taken during the 1950s. If we had a similar view today, in 2012, we would notice many changes with buildings demolished and rebuilt.

The Red Lion originally had its front door in Market Street but, for some reason, this was bricked up and the side door in Mealhouse Lane used as the main door. This photograph shows the pub in the early 1950s with the Town Hall Square visible in the distance.

Chorley Town Hall was completed in 1879 when the 'old' Town Hall was still in use opposite, at the end of Union Street, Chorley then having two Town Halls for a time. This view, taken in 1956, shows how many changes have taken place since then.

A late 1950s view of St Thomas's Road corner with Market Street. Note the cars on the former Town Hall Square with the Police Station behind.

Another Market Street corner, this time with Fazackerley Street. This photograph was taken when vehicles could turn either way when coming out of the street. Hereabouts were the Catholic Repository and Tootell's Tripe Shop. There was also Dunderdale's Thrift Stores, for whom the author delivered orders on a bicycle.

This time we are looking back towards the end of Fazackerley Street, from outside Mary Banks's shop. Note the old District Bank and the other shops, like Playfair and Griffiths.

Yet another street corner, and one which was about to change. This is the bottom end of Chapel Street. The building with scaffolding around it was Jardine's, with Seymour Mead's next door. This corner formed part of the so called 'Market Street Bulge'. It is pictured here in October 1955.

Another view of the corner of Chapel Street. The building was found to be unsafe and had to be demolished. The work is in progress in this view. Note how pedestrians had to walk in the road.

Looking up Market Street during the later 1950s, from F.W. Woolworth. The shop on Chapel Street corner has now been cleared. The first electric lights used to illuminate Market Street are still in place.

Looking towards F.W. Woolworth and the end of Fazackerley Street from the St Mary's Presbytery garden wall. Before Woolworth's is Williams Deacons Bank, prior to its rebuilding.

Viewed from the end of St George's Street is Market Street in the mid-1950s. Again it is the shops which bring back memories, especially so with those at the end of West Street. The old Co-op shop was there with Fairhurst's chemist's shop next door.

Moving past the end of St George's Street, this view shows the traffic queue extending to the end of Pall Mall corner. Next to the chemist's shop mentioned above was Bleasdale's, and across Parson's Brow was Halford's shop, an outlet much smaller than their new shop in Chorley.

This photograph was taken from the end of Halliwell Street with Halford's shop just visible to the right. Next door was the well-known sign, over Critchley's fish shop – 'If It Swims – We Have It'. The tall building in the centre of the picture is the Royal cinema. A Trent bus from the East Midlands is on its way to Blackpool.

Across the road from the Royal, we look towards the Town Hall in 1950s Market Street, with the Joiner's Arms at the end of Anderton Street and the Wellington at the bottom of Gillibrand Street.

From the end of Cunliffe Street, traffic is still queuing. On the corner of the street is the Cunliffe Arms. There are many changes to this scene today, though, as the mill chimney, St George's School, the shops by Cheapside and the travel agency have now all gone.

One of the rare occasions that Market Street was free of traffic. This mid-1950s view, at the end of Pall Mall, brings back memories of the old cast-iron 'Big Lamp' which used to stand here. It was replaced with a concrete lamp post, electrically lit, and just visible in this photograph.

Almost at the end of Albion Street, looking towards to the Plaza cinema 'up' Bolton Street. To the right is Back Street, where at this time the Fire Station and the Chorley Abattoir stood. Weekend traffic is queuing from the Town Hall to beyond the Plaza.

At the end of Standish Street, looking back to Market Street. It is hard to recall that there were shops on the forecourt of Chorley Ford. At the end of the street can be seen the King's Arms, later becoming part of Rimmers' car salesrooms.

In the text, I refer to an area nicknamed 'up Duke' – and this is it, at the Duke Street-Bolton Street crossroads, where the men all went, to 'traffic watch'. To quench thirsts, five pubs were close by, all visible in this photograph. Note the Plough Hotel, later to become the Borough.

Into Bolton Road now, and some of the old handloom weavers' cottages which stood on the east side. In this view, property between King Street and Queen Street East is shown.

Another view in Bolton Road, this time at the end of Princess Street. All this property was cleared away in 1957-58, including the King Street Lodging House.

CHURCHES AND SCHOOLS

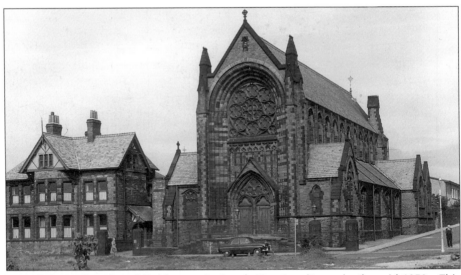

Sacred Heart Church and Presbytery, in Brook Street as it was in the mid-1950s. This photograph was taken from near the location where German bombs fell during World War Two. The site is now mostly built over.

The first schools photograph in this section was taken in 1949 and shows Duke Street School netball team of 60 years ago.

The 'school plot' at Duke Street School is the subject of this photograph which was taken in July of 1947. The girls seem busy enough, but where are the boys?

All Saints' Scout Group had a new hut built during 1956, which was dedicated by the Archdeacon of Blackburn. The hut was officially opened by Chorley's Mayor, Mr W. Lowe. The photograph shows dignatories and Scout leaders attending the official opening.

Another All Saints' view, this time taken outside the church in Moor Road. The Scouts and Cubs among the group add more interest to the photograph. Alas, the owner of the photograph cannot recall the occasion.

While in the Moor Road area, here is another view, this time taken at Southlands School in 1956. The occasion seems to be a trip or holiday somewhere, using the Leyland Royal Tiger coach. Caps and berets seem standard headgear.

This photograph was taken on Coppull Railway Station in the late 1950s and shows Preston Road Methodist Sunday School children's outing.

One's own primary school will always remain special in the memory. The author's was Hollinshead Street and this photograph shows the retirement of Miss Catterall in 1956 or 1957. Many will recall her with fondness, as will the Revd Storr also be recalled.

Two photographs of Chorley Parish Church 'Parish Tea Party' c.1955. The first photograph shows parishioners one side of the Town Hall Assembly Room and includes Cannon Wyatt. The second photograph shows parishioners at the other side of the room, including the author's Aunt Grace. Many friends and contemporaries are in these photographs.

Another photograph of Hollinshead Street School, this time in July 1956, the occasion being the presentation of the House Cup. The Revd and Mrs Storr are to the left, with the headmaster, Mr Firth, centre back.

The owner of this photograph is uncertain as to which Chorley school it features but the date may be 1956. The children appear to be be watching an eclipse, or perhaps sunspot activity.

The year 1958 saw a Mothers' Union Festival when representatives from local churches attended St James' for a special service. Some of those attendees are seen here waiting to enter the church.

The 1950s saw regular school cycle rallies. This one was in 1955, at Highfield School, the photograph being taken at the Brown Street gate into the schoolyard.

This photograph was probably taken during 1957, at a local school – although the owner is not sure which one – and illustrates the popularity of boys' caps.

The same unknown school and the same rally as shown in the previous photograph. This time the entrants seem a little apprehensive about the course being pointed out to them.

This picture is thought to have been taken in 1952 and the entrants to this cycle rally don't look in the least bit nervous of what is to come. The school has extension classrooms and may have been St Mary's, Duke Street or Highfield.

Pictured in the churchyard of St Mary's in 1950 is a class of girls. Many will recognise the headmaster Mr Bernard Grime, to the left. Many of the author's contemporaries are pictured, including Wynne Coyle on the front row.

We go out of town for this schooldays photograph, this time to Withnell. It was taken at Abbey Village School in 1951. One of the girls pictured here was a local councillor until May 1999.

St Chad's Church at South Hill, Whittle-le-Woods, has its origins in the 16th century, the present church having been regularly improved over the years. In March 1959, the Church was badly damaged by fire which destroyed the roof and other internal features, as pictured here.

INDUSTRIAL VIEWS

Canal boats were still being made in the Chorley area into the 1950s. One is shown here being launched from a boatyard at Riley Green The date of the photograph is August 1953.

Moving back to Chorley, this view was taken inside Edge's Diamond Mill, probably in June 1953 when the mill was decorated for the Queen's Coronation.

This Christmas party took place in the late 1950s. It was held at Lyons Lane Congregational Church Hall. The children were those of employees who worked at the Cowling Mill.

Another children's party, this one taking place in the canteen of Talbot Mill also during the late 1950s.

Many Chorley mills were still being driven by magnificent steam engines in the 1950s. At Talbot Mill were two engines, one driving the Spinning Mill, the other driving the Weaving Shed. The Shed engine is shown here.

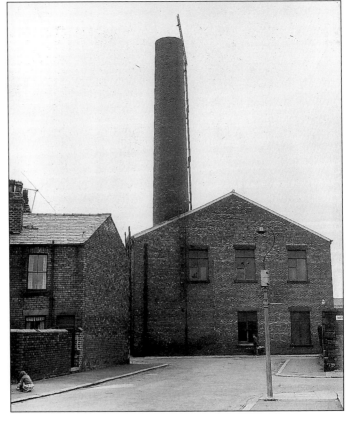

This was the gable end of Avenue Mill at the end of Hindley Street and Rydal Place, although the main entrance was from Longworth Street. It was last used by Thomas Witter & Co. New houses are built here today.

Another mill which was destroyed by fire during the later 1950s. This was in Crosse Hall Street. It had at least two names – Barkhouse and also Weir – and was quite old.

These 'Pit Brow' ladies are enjoying their Coronation party in 1953. It is uncertain which colliery this, is but it may be Welch Whittle Colliery. It is hard to believe that women worked on the 'Pit Brow' into the 1950s.

Another photograph of 'Pit Brow' women, this time sorting coal as it moves along a conveyor belt. It is July 1958 and the location is Welch Whittle Colliery.

Indirectly associated with industry were these local hostels. Three were built for ROF employees, but only two were used for this purpose. These were Woodlands in Southport Road, and Highways in Balshaw Lane. The latter is shown here from the adjoining station railway bridge.

At Chorley Royal Ordnance Factory, the end of the war saw a reduction in the labour force and in ammunition production. The post-war years saw the factory producing concrete house posts and panels, here being examined prior to removal to sites in places such as Euxton, Charnock Richard and Hoghton.

Another concrete product which was made at the ROF at Chorley into the 1950s was concrete railway sleepers. Many thousands of these were made due to the shortage of wood for sleepers. This view shows one of the two plants making the sleepers, on a 'continuous belt' system.

As the railway sleepers 'cured' (dried) in their mould, the reinforcing wires passing through them were cut off by burning, after which the sleepers were removed from their mould and dispatched countrywide.

The ROF had a 'Tailor's Shop' during the war years, and after the war, this went over to producing industrial clothing etc. This work continued well into the 1950s. In this view, the Tailor's Shop is decorated for the Coronation in 1953.

The longest lasting post-war work done at the ROF was the destruction of returned ammunition and one of many stacks is shown here. The ammunition was destroyed by detonating it and the noise from this process was the source of many complaints from local residents well into the 1950s.

The early 1950s saw a return to ammunition production at the ROF and more labour was recruited. Here, 3.5 inch rockets are being assembled.

By the mid-1950s, other post-war jobs had come to an end and the factory was back on full ammunition production. It was during the 1950s that the automatic filling of shells began as opposed to hand filling which had been done up to this time.

Outside Chorley for this view and to Adlington where a retirement presentation for Mrs A. Makinson, is under way. The photograph, at Brook Doubling Co Ltd, shows workmates at the presentation, in the 1950s.

The photograph of this accident at the end of Lancaster Street in Coppull also gives us a view of Coppull Ring Mill and Mavis Mill, just visible behind the chimney, which was shared by both mills.

Both the mills mentioned in the previous photograph were driven by J. & E. Wood engines. Here, the men who drove and looked after the engine at Coppull Ring Mill are pictured between the engine cylinders. The engine was similar to that preserved and running today at Trencherfield Mill, Wigan Pier.

Mavis Mill was demolished in the 1970s with no trace of it left today. But at least we have a photographic image of it here. To the right is the engine house with sprinkler water tower to the left.

On 14 October 1953, their Royal Highnesses, the Duchess of Kent and Princess Alexandra, visited Talbot Mills as part of a tour of the Lancashire textile industry. Here, the Duchess is seen with Mr Barber-Lomax, chairman of directors, in the Spinning Mill.

Here the Duchess of Kent is presented to Mrs H. Warburton, during their tour of the mill, whilst Princess Alexandra looks on.

In this view, Mr W.H. Morley shows Princess Alexandra a High Speed Beamer being operated by Miss Rhoda McDonald.

In the Bottom Ring Spinning Room of Talbot (or Bagganley) Mill, employee Mrs E. Mason is presented to HRH The Duchess of Kent by a monocled Mr Barber-Lomax.

At the end of their tour of Talbot Mill, their Royal Highnesses prepare to leave the cobbled mill yard with farewell hand shakes as some of the mill employees look on.

We began this section with a view of a canal boat and end with one as well. Here, a 1950s coal barge has sunk in Heath Charnock. No doubt a few buckets of coal would be removed by local residents. After all, it was a 'shipwreck' and the coal would be easier to collect than by 'kebbing'.

RAILWAYS

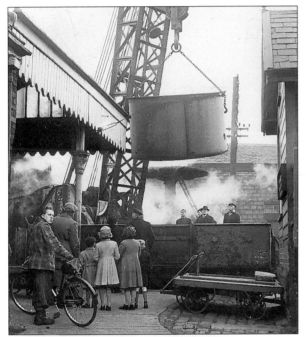

One graphic way to underline the end of steam locomotive working on our local lines is seen here. The photograph shows the removal of the water tank which was used to fill tenders of the engines. The photograph taken at Chorley Station in the late 1950s.

How it used to be on Chorley Railway Station during the July holidays. Here, in the later 1950s, the 'Preston Side' platform is full of intending passengers. Note the train in the 'bay' platform, for Blackburn. This took passengers via Heapey, Brinscall and Feniscowles.

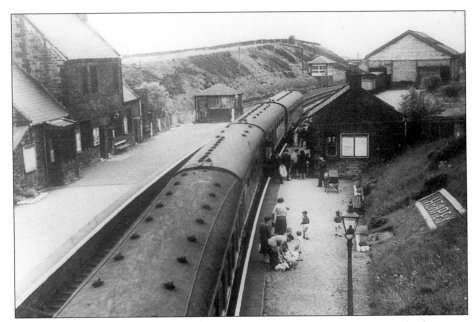

From Chorley, the Blackburn trains passed over Botany Viaduct and climbed to the first stop. This was Heapey Station, seen here from the road bridge, looking back towards Chorley and photographed in the 1950s.

The view from Stump Lane bridge looking towards Chorley Station in the mid-1950s. Note the Coal Yard to the left and a train on the Blackburn line.

From Coal Yard to Goods Yard. This hole in the wall of the Railway Street Goods Yard is alongside Lyons Lane Bridge and was caused by a road accident in 1957.

At least that hole in the wall, shown above, allowed one to see into the Goods Yard. The photograph looks into an area which has now become the town centre bypass. Chorley Station is to the centre right.

Another view of the Railway Street Goods Yard, this time showing the large wooden warehouse used for storing goods received and prior to dispatch. Incidentally, the office building in the centre was built on the site of Chorley's original railway station in the 1840s.

Remember the Chorley Goods Depot and their delivery and collection vehicles? These were Scammell Scarabs and were three-wheelers. Chorley had about a half dozen of them on local work. The photograph shows a presentation to the drivers in the Goods Yard.

This is another photograph which could not be repeated today. It is the entrance to the Goods Yard from the corner of Railway Street and Lyons Lane. It certainly shows the difference compared to the same location today.

The owner of this photograph is uncertain as to its location. It could be at either Coppull or Balshaw Lane Stations, for they were both very similar. The author thinks it is the latter. Photographed about 1958, the group are cup winners it seems, but for what?

Staying out of town, this is Lower Adlington, photographed from the railway bridge at White Bear Station on the former Wigan-Blackburn line looking towards the A6 road bridge. The Waiting Room on the left-hand platform is all that remains today. The line was closed in the 1960s.

Under Stump Lane Bridge, a WD 2-8-0 is on an engineers' train.

Two photographs taken in February 1958. The train was stuck in snow at Grimeford Cutting near Adlington. The first photograph shows a distant view of the train, which was bound for Bolton. The second, closer to the engine, shows the men still smiling, despite having to dig the snow away. The engine is a 'Black-Five', number 45206.

Spotters at Chorley Station in the early 1950s regularly saw the same engines, which led to plenty of moans. This was one of the regulars through Chorley on goods work. It was photographed in September 1952, coming from Stump Bridge.

Here we see yet another 'workhorse' on the Blackburn line. This is a WD 2-8-0 number 90419 from shed 26D. The engine also seems to be on an engineer's train, but this time has a bowler-hatted man on the footplate.

The shape of things to come! Here we see one of the first of the DMUs (Diesel Multiple Units) to stop at Chorley Station. The date of the photograph is believed to be towards the end of the 1950s.

The Chorley area had many railway branches serving works such as Heapey and Dacca Twist as well as collieries such as Welch Whittle, Ellerbeck and Chisnall. Coal trains were made up in sidings, such as Hic Bibi, Coppull, where our photograph shows a crash between road and rail wagons.

COACH OUTINGS

The Royal Ordnance Factory near Chorley reduced its workforce from the war years from 30,000 or so to a few thousand in the post-war years. In the 1950s it employed about 5,000. It also organised annual coach trips for employees' children, as shown here on the Flat Iron about 1956.

The location is Railway Street in the later 1950s. The group shown are about to leave on the coach for a week end at Cliff College, Calver, Derbyshire. Former Hollinshead Street School contemporaries of the author are included here, including Pam Greenway and James Welch.

The end of Pall Mall, this time, probably in 1956. The trip getting ready to leave is for the children of the RAOB ('Buffaloes') in Chorley.

The trip on this occasion was one organised by residents of two Chorley streets, Seymour Street and Longton Street. The coaches are destined for Blackpool Illuminations in the later 1950s. Street outings were typical of the decade.

Remember the Town Hall Square behind the Town Hall? The coach shown here is parked there. The destination of the outing is not known, but the date is about 1957. Note the labels on the childrens' coats, reminiscent of evacuees during the war.

This later 1950s photograph was also taken on the Flat Iron. The building behind the bus contained cattle pens. Later, the Gas Showrooms were here. The group includes Mr and Mrs Harrison formerly of Common Bank Farm, so the outing may have had farming associations.

This is another ROF outing, probably in 1958. This time, though, the destination is Blackpool Tower Circus.

The location of this photograph is Clifford Street, outside the Labour Party Office, and the trip is believed to for the Chorley Labour Party League of Youth and pictured in the late 1950s.

Taken during the late 1950s, possibly 1958, this photograph is of another happy band of young travellers but, alas, their identity is not known.

Pictured in Willow Road on Thornhill, this coach outing is taking North Ward Labour Party children on a trip to Southport in the late 1950s.

During the 1950s, many local firms laid on trips for employees' children. Ribble Motors' Chorley Depot was among these. This photograph on the Flat Iron was taken in 1959 or 1960.

About two years later another Ribble trip, in 1962, is photographed in front of the Baths on the Flat Iron. Note the wonderful Royal Tiger buses which were also used on express routes. This trip is pictured before leaving for Belle Vue.

This group of Euxton pensioners are about to leave on their annual trip, this time to Chester during mid-1962.

THAT'S ENTERTAINMENT

The only association this photograph has with the subject of this book is the children, for by the 1950s most of them would have 'come of age' and be in their 20s. But the photograph is rare and worthy of inclusion. It shows the demolition of the Royal Oak in 1937, and the start of the Mickey Mouse Club at the new Odeon.

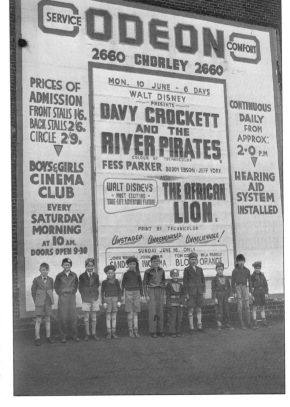

Another view taken alongside the Odeon, when 'Davy Crockett' hats were all the rage during 1957. Note the 'one-up-one-down' sock style the lads have adopted.

This view of Chorley Odeon's auditorium will revive pleasant memories for all those who remember this cinema in the 1950s. This was one of the 'posh' cinemas many people reserved for Saturday nights. Alas, the photograph does not show the decorated plasterwork.

The foyer of the Odeon was used to advertise the Ideal Home Exhibition at Chorley Town Hall, linking it with the Norman Wisdom film, *One Good Turn*.

Another advertisement, this time pictured in the Plaza cinema foyer. It advertised drinks from T. & R. Smiths, a Chorley soft drinks manufacturer. Again the title of the film being shown, this time *The Sun Also Rises*, starring Tyrone Power, Errol Flynn and Ava Gardner, was worked into the advert.

This event took place on the Flat Iron during the late 1950s. It was quite spectacular when the performance took place in the evening, when it was getting dark.

PEOPLE

Pictured in Regent Road adjoining Chorley Barracks, this group of Territorial Army servicemen appear to be looking forward to their forthcoming camp in May 1955.

A sad event in April 1958. An RSPCA plaque is being presented posthumously to a dog called Rex for saving the life of a three-year-old child in Coppull.

Finalists in the Model Girl competition held in the Odeon Theatre in the late 1950s. The winners are to the left side of the line up. They are, in order of their winning position, first Ruth Lathom, second June Rance and third Margaret Monks.

Competitors, and apparently winners, at Blackpool Music Festival were this group of young ladies who were pupils of Mrs J. McIntosh of Coppull. CADOS regulars will recognise Wynne Tootall in the centre of the picture.

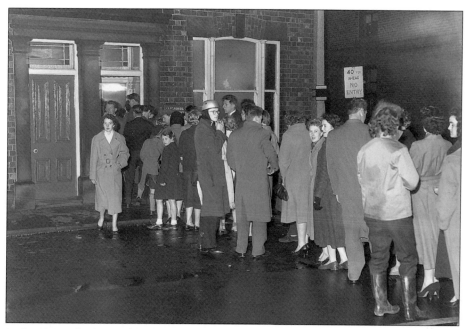

In the 1950s, Chorley Health Clinic was on the Town Hall Square. These people are queuing to receive the polio vaccine after a nationwide outbreak of the disease.

A pram race taking place at Johnny's Brow, Crosse Hall. Nearest the camera appears to be a team from a Scout Troop. The M61 motorway passes under this spot today, a bridge now replaces the road shown above.

In the late 1950s, with the clearance of old property in Bolton Street and other streets adjoining it, one of the buildings to be cleared was the King Street Lodging House. The men living there, shown here, had to be relocated to Moorfields Hospital on Eaves Lane.

The coming to Chorley of Sunday cinema opening happened only after a poll was conducted in the Town Hall Assembly Room. No doubt many will recognise Mr Arthur Rigby to the left.

Remember the wallpaper shop of Miller's, at the corner of New Market Street and Hill Street, with its later additional shop across the road? Here, staff and relatives pose in the shop doorway, prior to an outing in 1954 or 1955. Note the men's gabardine 'macs' and trouser turn-ups.

During 1953, a local archaeological society was formed. The first 'dig' was at Bretters Farm, Heath Charnock. The photograph shows, from the left, chairman Alderman C. Williams, secretary J. Winstanley, an unknown member and treasurer Jack Smith, the author of this book.

Although the owner of this photograph does not recall the occasion, we do know that it was in the mid-1950s and in Chorley. And a least we can see what fashions were typical of the time.

This 1958 photograph shows members of the Chorley Branch of the Girls' Training Corps. The event is a presentation, thought to have been taking place in Chorley Barracks in Devonshire Road.

The banner in this photograph, taken in the mid-to-late 1950s in Chorley, speaks for itself. The Revd Storr from Hollinshead Street Church will be fondly recalled by many.

Pictured in the Public Baths which were on the Flat Iron, some of those in this mid-1950s group are Mrs C. Monks, Mr R. Rigby, and the Baths Superintendent of the time. The nature of the event is not known, however.

With the swimming baths theme in mind, another pool is shown here. This is at a Butlin's holiday camp in 1958. All the holidaymakers on the photograph are from Chorley.

Astley Park in the 1950s, one of the best locations for sledging in the Chorley area. The length of run was from the car park railings of today, across the main drive and down the hill to 'jump' the River Chor at the bottom – considered a true Chorleyite's baptism. Of course, many brave souls often finished in the river itself.

We move into the early 1960s in this photograph which shows members of Chorley Civil Defence Corps. The group at this time used to practise rescue work with army personnel at ROF Chorley at weekends.

Again, the nature and date of this photograph is not known but it appears to be either an outing or is maybe a bowls team pictured on their green. It is believed to be from the early 1960s.

This group, outside the Baptist Chapel in St George's Street, were photographed in early 1962, about to leave for a trip to the Lake District. The author's Aunt Grace (Nixon) is second from the left, standing.

DANCES AND PARTIES

The Corinthians hockey team, who are also featured in the Sporting Days chapter, are here pictured with friends and other attendees at a dance at the Tudor in Gillibrand Street.

Another dance at the Tudor in the late 1950s. It was usual at this dance hall to hold private dances on a Friday evening, tickets only. On Saturday, it was was 'pay at the door'. When the Tudor Dance Club was formed a membership card had to be produced for Sunday night dances.

Many regular attenders of the Saturday night dances are seen in this photograph, again in the Tudor. Bert Barker's Band was resident here.

The Tudor yet again, and a photograph taken at a private dance for Chorley Football Club supporters, probably in 1957. Again several contemporaries of the author are among those attending this dance.

This time it is the turn of the Chorley Alliance Cricket League to hold their annual dance at the Tudor in the mid-1950s.

Another venue for dancing in Chorley was the Ambulance Hall, where this group of young dancers are pictured in 1958.

A Christmas dance during the later 1950s, probably at the Tudor again.

Although pictured in a Blackpool dance hall, the people were from Chorley. The occasion was the Cyril Lord factory dance. This factory was off Seymour Street and was known as Greenfield or Co-op Mill.

Just out of town for this group of dancers, to Adlington in fact, where the Parish Church Christmas dance is taking place.

This time we are at Eccleston and the occasion is the local football club dance competition held in the church hall during the later 1950s.

July 1948 and a garden party at St John's Church in Coppull. Sitting in the centre back is the Rose Queen, Evelyn Lane. The choirboys each side of her are Bob Bolton and John Lane.

It is believed that this group is Lyons Lane Oddfellows childrens' Christmas party, pictured during the later 1950s.

How about this for wall-to-wall grimaces and smiles? There are some memorable faces here, all 200 or so of them! Taken in 1958, the photograph is of St Anselm's Church Christmas party.

This Christmas party group in Adlington was, it is believed, photographed in 1958. No other details are known.

Annual school dances always had their 'traumas of the heart'. It is Christmas 1958 and the group are from Chorley Southlands School.

It is thought that this photograph was taken at the Perrite Works Christmas party but the date is uncertain.

This group of ladies attended a dance at Chorley Town Hall in the 1950s. Again, it is interesting to note the fashion of the era.

Yet another dance at the Town Hall. This time it was the turn of White Coppice Cricket Club during the later 1950s.

This photograph was taken at the dance and party of Messrs Underhills of Steeley Lane about 1960, according to the owner of the print.

PARADES

These next three photographs were taken within minutes of each other during the same parade, on St George's Day in 1958 in Market Street. The Girl Guides are passing the end of West Street.

Now it is the turn of the Boy Scouts to pass the camera in the same location. At least two of the author's contemporaries are pictured – boyhood friend Roy Barker and Albert Darlington, son of the man who ran a barber's shop under Victoria Arcade.

The same parade but a different location in Market Street, this time at the bottom of Chapel Street. In the background is St Mary's Presbytery gardens and Williams Deacon's Bank before it was rebuilt to become the Royal Bank of Scotland.

A Remembrance Day parade in the later 1950s passes Chorley Parish Church, with Mayor and Councillors wearing their robes and hats.

A Church Lads' Brigade parade in 1957, this time located on the Flat Iron in the Market Place. We are looking towards the south end of the Flat Iron with the backs of property in Livesey Street visible. Note Messrs Haydock's sawmill with chimney, to the left. All this property has now disappeared.

The same parade as pictured in the previous photograph, this time showing an inspection of the younger element taking place. New recruits, still waiting for their uniforms, appear to be making up part of the parade.

This photograph of the Church Lads' Brigade Band in St Thomas's Road in the late 1950s will, I know, evoke discussion among former Brigade members who have spoken to the author about band members. There is some dispute about who was in the band on this occasion.

Another Church Lads' Brigade parade, this time in 1958. In this view to the north, Union Street is in the background with Hughlock Hindle's garage standing where today's Civic Building now stands.

This mid-1950s photograph shows another Mayoral procession entering Chorley Parish Churchyard. Of course, at that time the building across Market Street from the church gates was the Central Conservative Club.

Coronation Recreation Ground in Devonshire Road is the setting for this photograph as the Mayor and other dignatories, including Mr Roy Fisher, take the salute from the passing parade.

The same parade as this time Boy Scouts pass the saluting platform. Leading them is the brother of Roy Barker, mentioned in an earlier photograph caption (page 129).

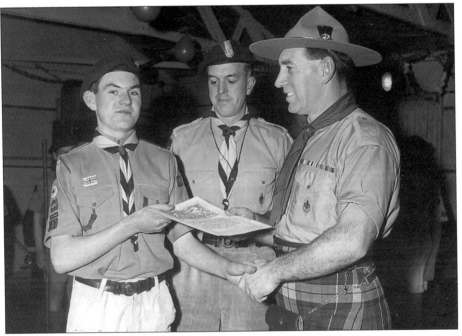

Roy Fisher, on the right, presents a King's Scout award. In the centre is Mr Keith Barker. Three members of the Barker family were closely associated with the Boy Scout movement in Chorley.

Another parade, another year. This time Girl Guides pass by the saluting base on Coronation Rec in the mid-1950s.

A rather small contingent of Sea Scouts passes through Coronation Rec during the same parade as in the previous photograph, thought to be in 1956. The former St Mary's Hall is just visible to the left.

A Mayoral procession in either Chapel Street or Parker Street in about 1961.

CARNIVALS AND CROWNINGS

The first-ever Chorley Round Table Charity Carnival was held in the late 1950s and a section of the carnival parade is pictured here in cobbled Devonshire Road. Some of the houses in this location have been demolished due to mining subsidence.

The same carnival as in the previous photograph, this time with a Ford Thames van, owned by Mr Clare, plumber and glazier of Eaves Lane, dressed up for the procession around the town. It is advertising the RAFA Wing's day appeal.

Still in the Borough of Chorley, here is an Adlington Carnival Queen's float in the 1950s.

Young girls sitting around the maypole during an Adlington Carnival procession.

This photograph of Lower Adlington Morris Dancers has evoked several questions about the troop. They are seen here close to the carnival field before taking part in a dancing competition.

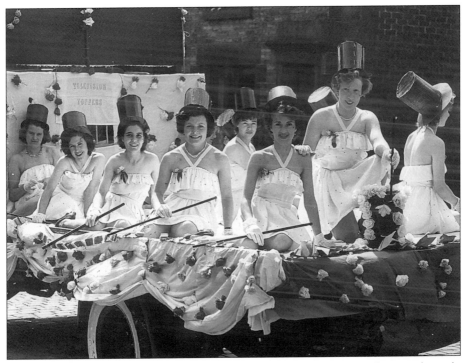

This 'Television Toppers' float is perhaps a reminder of what we were watching on the early television shows of the 1950s.

Mr and Mrs Fairclough with the Rivington and Adlington Band. The occasion is not known.

A May Queen with her attendants outside a Chorley church in the 1950s.

Miss M. Hibbert performs the crowning of the May Queen who is, of course, the same young lady pictured in the previous photograph.

The banner says it all – 'Heapey and Wheelton Coronation Festival Queen' – so the photograph must presumably have been taken in 1953.

HEAPEY & WHEEL
CORONATION FESTIVAL QU

A young looking Ken Dodd together with the Mayor of Chorley and the Carnival Queen are all together on the stage built on Coronation Rec in 1958.

Carnival Queen or May Queen? Another 1950s event, this time thought to be in Coppull. The double-decker bus in the background is advertising 'Progress and Turner's Tours'.

The same venue as in the previous photograph but a slightly different location as the carnival parade passes. In fact the Ladywell Eldorado Prize Jazz Band is going past. Coppull Bandroom appears to be in the upper right of the picture.

Yet another of those puzzling 'no information' photographs, showing another 'queen' with attendants. Taken in the later 1950s, it has been suggested that the occasion is something to do with St Peter's Church.

A Chorley Carnival Queen receives her trophy from the Mayor, watched by the runners-up and the Mayoress.

Chorley's Carnival Queen of 1962, pictured with Miss Morecambe and Miss Great Britain Bathing Beauty.

The runners-up for the Chorley Carnival Queen crown in 1962. Both are seen here about to set off in the carnival procession.

WALKING DAYS

In the Coronation Year of 1953, Walking Day was celebrated moreso with flags and bunting. Leading the procession were St Peter's. The girls carrying the 'E II R' banner, were Pauline Kitching, Ann Whittam and Ann Simmonds. The two girls on the outside wore royal blue and white, and in the middle, a white dress.

A 1959 or 1960 picture of St George's girls' passing the end of Fazackerley Street. Note the shops. To the left is Thorps and Broughs with Wilcocks at the end of the street. To the right is Reuben Marsden's, Partnership Supply Co and the *Chorley Guardian* offices.

Getting the children ready was a job for the ladies at the ends of the rope lines. Here, the same group as that pictured in the previous photograph are got ready in St George's Schoolyard.

This time it is the turn of the boys of St George's to be lined up and told to 'keep hold of the rope'.

These two photographs show groups of both boys and girls, but it seems that overall the girls were pictured more often. Perhaps the boys were too shy?

Once again it is the girls who steal the limelight in these two photographs. Perhaps it was simply because they were more photogenic.

It is a pity that these photographs are not in colour, for in black and white they do not do justice to the dresses and the flowers. In the second photograph it is unusual to see both boys and girls pictured together.

All Saints' children are being got ready. Like St Peter's, All Saints' children had longer to walk than most even to reach the town centre. In those days, many more people liked to watch the church parades than do today.

As a mission chapel under St George's, the children from Red Bank in Carr Lane assembled in St George's Schoolyard. Although the banner behind the children in this photograph says 'Bank', it is not certain if the children themselves attended Red Bank mission.

Moving out of the town for a few more Walking Day photographs, here in Euxton some of the girls from the Parish Church are shown just before starting on their walk through the village.

I am told this was either Euxton or Eccleston. It is certainly a gem of a picture, especially as it shows the boys with all those scrubbed knees and neatly parted hair. Today they'll all be into middle age, of course.

Moving to Heapey here are the girls of St Barnabas's Parish Church, walking in front of their Sunday School banner.

Wrightington was part of Chorley's rural area in the 1950s, although today it seems to be more associated with Wigan. This photograph shows some of the girls from St James's Parish Church there.

In the first picture the girls from St Mary's Parish Church in Eccleston walk along the main street in front of their banner. In the second, boys from the same church feature, complete with short trousers and, in some cases, caps.

Girls from Coppull Parish Church of St John the Divine en route through the village on their Walking Day.

To Whittle-le-Woods and in Whittle Bottoms we see the Walking Day procession from St John's Parish Church in either 1961 or 1962.

Returning to Chorley for the last Walking Day photographs and members of St Laurence's Parish Church Choir prepare to start out on their walk outside the Boys' School in Parker Street.

The same venue as the previous photograph and here some of the girls who will be taking part in the procession about to start. Both these photographs are thought to date from about 1960, but it could be earlier.

In 1962, at the corner of Eaves Lane and Harper's Lane, children from St Peter's Church are about to set off on their long walk into town.

A 1962 Walking Day procession passes the end of St Thomas's Road. Two very smart young boys are carrying the banner.

INCIDENTS AND ACCIDENTS

Pictured in Park Road about July 1960, an articulated wagon of Northern Ireland Trailers Ltd has jackknifed between Millfield and Highfield Roads. The rather minor accident has attracted the usual onlookers.

A policeman is on traffic control duty at the end of Queen's Road, due to resurfacing work going on from here to Chapel Street in 1957. Note the Anne Pollard water fountain to the right of the policeman, and the Parish Church Institute further along Park Road.

The road works mentioned in the previous photograph continue in front of the Town Hall. To the left is Messrs Stone's shop. The bicycle outside reminds the author of when he rode it to make deliveries.

To the left is the old Barclay's Bank building at the corner of High Street. Across Market Street was Reuben Marsden's shop – and still the road works continue.

There is plenty going on in this photograph, also dating from about 1957. We see Market Street and Fazackerley Street corner. There seems to be a fire close by together with the usual crowd of onlookers. The delivery cycle from Stone's shop is in the centre of the picture, its rider weaving his way past a policeman and hose pipes.

It is 1957 and an unusually wide load negotiates the wrong side of the road as it squeezes past the Town Hall. Thankfully, Market Street is now free of such traffic.

This mid-1950s view shows Fazackerley Street corner with Market Street, before traffic changes were introduced. A Jaguar appears to be the worse for wear after a collision and is being made ready to be towed away. Again the shops may be of interest to readers.

At the infamous crossroads of Duke Street and Lyons Lane with Bolton Street and Road, a traffic survey is under way, prior to the fitting of traffic lights. This was December 1958. Note the Princess Royal pub and Plaza cinema across the street.

Following the survey of traffic using the Duke Street crossroads, the first traffic lights were installed 'on trial only' during 1959. Council officials and police watch the operation on an early winter's evening with smoke and fog threatening in the background.

Surveying traffic seemed to be popular in the 1950s. This survey is taking place in front of Yarrow House in September 1956. The reason for the census was to provide facts in advance of a town bypass, although the scene looks a bit like a customs check on some European border.

The same census location as the previous photograph. Here we see the traffic stretching back past the Yarrow Bridge pub and up the hill towards Wigan Lane. There are a few interesting 1950s cars here as well, their drivers as yet to face a questionnaire at the census point.

We move back to Park Road, in 1956, and a collision is attracting the attention of the public with the police keeping a watchful eye on traffic passing the scene at the end of Wellington Street.

On Wigan Road, Euxton, during the later 1950s, a flood occurred outside Euxton Institute, causing traffic problems and the need for fire-engines to remove the water. The main A49 road had to cope with all the traffic flowing through Euxton. The first photograph shows the flood at a distance The second gives a closer view with a coach from Stoke-on-Trent passing by.

Stranded passengers on the Rivington 312 service found that they really had to 'get out and push'. But their efforts were in vain and the bus had to be removed with the aid of the Ribble garage tow truck. Note the height of snow behind the bus, with boys standing on top of it.

The location is Rivington during the later 1950s. It took some time to clear the roads and many accidents ensued.

It is hard to believe that the A6 trunk road junction had no traffic lights until the late 1950s. This view is looking towards Chorley from the Adlington side of Skew Bridge, Heath Charnock. An accident waiting to happen...?

MAINLY ABOUT CARS

We certainly have not left behind the subject of accidents, although in the 1950s, car crashes were still sufficiently uncommon – there was, after all, less traffic – to attract a crowd. Here a damaged Jowett Javelin is parked in front of a police Mk II Ford Zodiac.

Although looking at cars here, this view, taken from the Imperial Hotel in Union Street, gives us a panorama of buildings which have nearly all gone today – the mills, chimneys, baths, Clifford Street and Brunswick Street houses, etc, have all disappeared. The Flat Iron market remains though.

Another view on the Flat Iron, looking back to the Imperial pub from where the previous photograph was taken. The pub is between Brimley's leather works and Hughlock Hindle's garage.

Yet another view of this Union Street location and Hughlock Hindle's garage. Just beyond the garage can be seen Dennerley's pawnbroker's shop.

This 1959 view of a garage saleroom shows an interesting selection of cars, priced between £300 and £700. They are an Austin Somerset soft top, Singer Gazelle, Hillman, Austin, Ford Popular, Hillman, MG, and a Morris van.

Yet another accident, this time at the Wigan Lane-Bolton Road corner. At this time, c.1959, there were no traffic lights at the Wigan Lane end, possibly a reason for the accident. To the left are the two vehicles involved, one of them from the Withy Trees Corn Mill at Bamber Bridge.

Another view of the vehicle involved in the accident in the previous photograph. If it had survived, this lorry would be a collector's item today.

This MG saloon car had suffered front-end damage due to a collision with a van belonging to the Hygienic Laundry during March 1962.

And here is that van. The Hygienic Laundry was one of two laundries in Chorley, the other being Brigg's.

Back to the Flat Iron for this photograph, also taken during 1962. The car is a Sunbeam Talbot which is taking part in Chorley Carnival Rally. The 'CAC' at the top of the board stating 'CHECK', refers to Chorley Automobile Club, the organisers of the rally.

Yet another 1962 photograph, this time taken in Standish Street. Here the cars – all Ford Anglias – are taking part in Bradshaw's Team Rally.

Also pictured in Standish Street, in 1961 or 1962, are cars for sale on the car park of Bradshaw's, as Chorley Ford dealership was called at the time. There are Populars, Anglias, Prefects, Austin A40s, Vauxhall Wyverns and Victors.

Yet another part of Bradshaw's yard is seen here. Some of the cars for sale include Austins, MGs, Bedford Dormobiles, Morrises and Hillmans. A new Ford Zodiac Mk III is in the street.

A Rover has wrapped itself around a lamppost at Clayton Green during the later 1950s. Note the traffic lights at this crossroads.

Early 1962 saw the completion of a new car showrooms in Bolton Street for Messrs Marsh of Chorley, suppliers of Humber, Hillman, Sunbeam and Commer vehicles. In 1999 the building was refurbished.

The opening of Britain's first motorway, then called the Preston bypass, was performed by Prime Minister Harold Macmillan in December 1958.

These photographs of the same accident were taken in Lyons Lane in the early 1950s. A Humber car appears to have crashed into houses between Brook Street and Castle Street. The first picture looks towards Brook Street, The second is looking toward Lyons Lane railway bridge. In the 40-plus years since these photographs were taken, the area has changed a great deal; all the houses have gone and a new road built where they stood.

CELEBRITY VISITORS

Our first two celebrities to visit Chorley in the mid-1950s were both great supporters of fund raising for the mentally handicapped. They were Harry Korris (left), of radio fame, and Hylda Baker (right), well-known for her television appearances and her catch-phrase, "She Knows You Know!"

The Royal Oak Hotel in Chorley was a popular venue for official functions in the 1950s. Here we see Councillor Gaskell, Mayor of Chorley, presenting a silver casket to comedian Charlie Chester at the Chorley Hospital Welfare Ball during 1955.

How many readers remember 'Musical Marie'? She was from Bolton and at the Royal in Market Street, she played day and night in an attempt to beat a piano playing record.

Although the owner of this photograph does not know the identity of the visiting celebrity seen here signing an autograph book, the venue was definitely Cooper's towel factory in 1955.

Stars such as Anna Neagle and Jimmy Hanley visited the Odeon. Here, the Odeon manager looks on while his son presents flowers to a celebrity visitor.

The first singer to be featured at the number-one spot when national popular music charts began in 1952 was Al Martino. He visited Chorley during 1956, when the venue was Stewart Porter's in Market Street. Here the singer is signing autographs for fans.

Another photograph of Al Martino at Stewart Porter's, this time putting one of his records on the radiogramme turntable. As a matter of interest, over 40 years later this particular radiogramme was alive and well and living in Euxton.

Popular singer Frankie Vaughan came to Chorley during 1956, when he performed at the Town Hall. He is seen here surrounded by the audience during his performance. Not much room for him to 'kick' here is there?

Another photograph of Frankie Vaughan at the Town Hall. This time, he seems to be singing for two particular young ladies leaning over the piano, He was an artist who did a great amount of work for young people and was a great supporter of the Boys' Club organisation.

I'm sure no one will need to be reminded who this celebrity visitor is, at a Chorley factory. He did quite a lot of television, mostly on panel game shows. Yes, it is a young Bob Monkhouse.

Radio brought Lancashlre's Jimmy Clitheroe to fame and fortune. He did some television work as well during its earlier years. He is seen here at a function in Chorley in 1957.

Singer Eden Kane visits Chorley Plaza during October 1961. He was one of the large number of young performers who came to prominence during the late 1950s revolution in popular music.

1962 saw at least two celebrities visiting Chorley. One of these was television 'straight man' Nicholas Parsons, seen here to the right of the photograph, along with the Chorley Carnival Queen and the Mayor and Mayoress.

With the advent of television, TV stars began to visit the town in the later 1950s, *Coronation Street* actors being particularly popular choices to open new shops or fêtes. Here is the *Street's* Lucille Hewit signing autographs, c.1962.

Guy Mitchell and Dorothy Holgate listen to one of the star's records at the farmhouse at Abbey Village.

When a fan's dream became reality

By mid-September 1955, Dorothy Holgate from Gerrards Fold Farm, in Abbey Village had been to see her singer idol 17 times since first watching him at Blackpool after he had come over to tour the UK from the USA.

They became good friends, exchanging letters and gifts, and in one of her letters, Dorothy invited the singer to visit her parents' farm. To her surprise – and not a little apprehension – a letter came saying that the singer would come to Abbey Village when he was next in the area, playing in Manchester.

That singer was Guy Mitchell, who arrived in the village in a large American car. The management at Abbey Mill requested that he be kept away from the area around the mill as they feared that production would suffer when adoring fans left their workplaces to see their idol.

Guy, who was an accomplished horseman, went riding with Dorothy, on horses from a Bury Lane, Withnell, stable. He spent the whole day at the farm and certainly made a dream come true for one young Chorley area girl.

To the envy of her friends and fans alike, Dorothy Holgate prepares to go horse riding with Guy Mitchell.

Ready for the off. Dorothy Holgate, Guy Mitchell and the owner of the stables, which adjoined Withnell Hall.

STREETS AND BUILDINGS

Those who fished at the pond at Chorley Hall will certainly recognise this location, but today it has been built over. This view looks east towards Preston Road where the Comet store now stands. The chimney in the distance belonged to Smethurst's North Street Mill.

The same mill and chimney as in the previous photograph, but this time looking from the bottom of Preston Street in the 1950s, when the site of today's B & Q store was used as part of an adjoining scrapyard.

This photograph was taken during the building of Thornhill Council Estate in the 1950s, although the car looks to be of an earlier vintage.

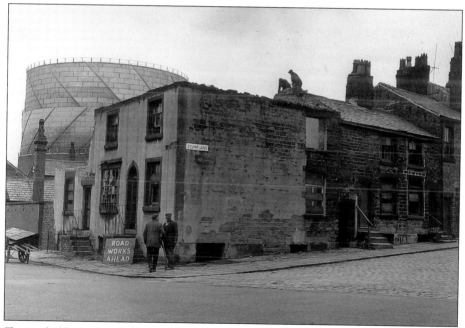

The gas holder easily identifies this location. It is the end of Stump Lane at its junction with Clifford Street, Bengal Street and Hollinshead Street. Some of the property on the corner is being demolished.

Continuing down Hollinshead Street in the 1950s there was an old building where today's Civic Buildings car park now stands. This was known as Hollinshead House and adjoined Brimley's Leather Works. Here it is being demolished in 1958.

At the west end of Hollinshead Street, at its junction with Church Brow, were house numbers 1-3, shown here in 1957. They later became derelict and almost demolished but eventually became The Swan with Two Necks.

In the first picture, from the the mid-1950s, we are looking up Church Brow from the two houses shown in the previous photograph. This road used to be a great run for sledges or four wheeled bogies – although a bit too fast for some! In the second photograph, a better view of the Parish Church is obtained with the old doorway to the left.

Moving back to Clifford Street in the later 1950s, in this photograph, looking south, a Ford Popular is coming out of Union Street. But the most remarkable thing about the picture is that over 90 per cent of the buildings are gone and the town centre bypass is here now.

Looking the other way from the previous photograph, we can see at the end of Union Street, the Rendezvous Café which was very popular on market days, although on a 'blind' corner, especially for buses turning into Clifford Street. The café was eventually demolished and Union Street made wider.

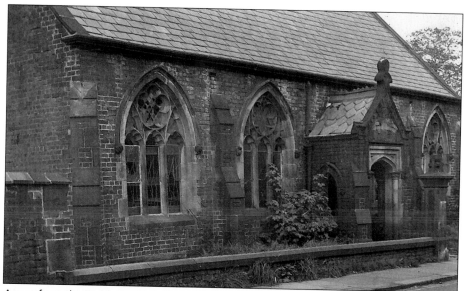

Across from the Parish Church is Queen's Road. And a short distance along that road, where Astley Park car park is today, stood this building into the 1950s. It was the second Grammar

School, built in Chorley in the 1860s. This is the Grammar School which was attended by a young Herbert Lightoller, the senior surviving officer when the *Titanic* sank 100 years ago this year. Lightoller was born in Chorley.

A closer look at the doorway of the old Grammar School, through which many of the town's worthies of the 19th century would pass through daily. The porch was a place where, as boys, the author and his pals would often shelter from the rain, while planning their next 'campaign'.

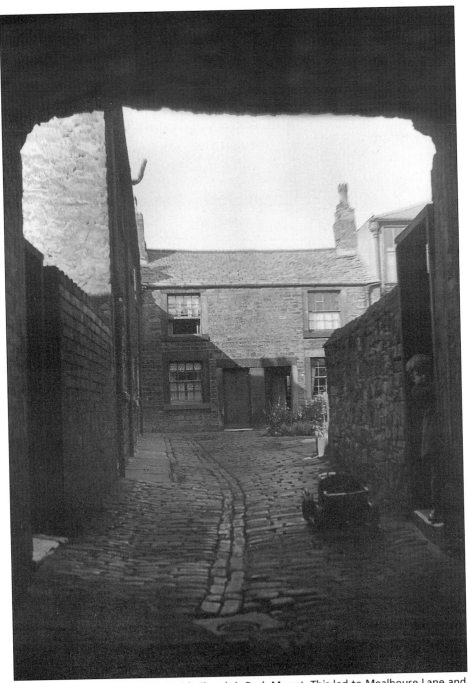

Across Market Street from the Parish Church is Back Mount. This led to Mealhouse Lane and Town Hall Square. At the top of the 'Mount' itself was an archway leading to a courtyard of old cottages, which can be seen in this photograph.

Also in Back Mount were the last 'one-up-one-down' cottages in Chorley, three of them in fact, as shown in this photograph. This was an area the author knew well, living close by and often going into them. All three cottages shared one backyard with one outside toilet. They were demolished in the early 1960s.

Next to the cottages in Back Mount was the Red Lion 'Tap', seen here about 1960. It was connected to the main Red Lion pub at the end of Mealhouse Lane by a courtyard. The White Hart was built on the Red Lion site in the early 1960s.

The last of the old properties to be demolished in Union Street was the shop of Chorley's pawnbroker, Messrs Dennerley, seen here about 1954. Note the side wall of the Odeon to the right-hand side.

This is another early 1950s photograph showing the demolition of the old Dennerley's pawnbroker's shop in Union Street. The parish churchyard is to the left, just out of the picture.

Next to the shop shown in the previous picture was an alleyway, the shop to one side, the Parish Church wall to the other. Here the churchyard wall is put to good use by pupils from the Grammar School in Union Street during the 1950s.

An interesting view from the Grammar School steps opposite the bus station, taken at end of the 1950s. Note the buildings in the distance. All of them have gone today, including seven factory chimneys and Brown Street Mill.

Brown Street Mill is just visible behind this house which was the home of the former mill owner, Mr Brown. It stood – where else? – in Brown Street! The house was derelict at the time of the photograph but was restored to become the first Chorley Boys' Club in the early 1950s.

The Victoria Building in Cleveland Street not only accommodated the Victoria Dance Hall (the Vic) on the top floor, it also had an arcade. The shop on the corner, Sharples, had a famous slogan: 'If it comes from a loom – try Sharples first.'

Into Chapel Street now, at its junction with Cleveland Street looking towards Market Street.
Note the shops of the time, pictured in the mid-1950s: Burton's, Dewhurst's George Mason's,
Zip Cleaners, Diane, County Meat Co, and Seymour Mead's.

Still in Chapel Street, this time looking the other way. Again it is the shops which catch the
eye, names such as Turner's, Kennedy's, Ball's, Melia's and Stylo at the corner of New Market
Street.

Higher up Chapel Street, looking back down the same side as the previous photograph, this time from the end of Church Street to New Market Street. Many ladies will recall Madame Edith's hairdressers. Then there are Pennine Cleaners, Leone's, Winter and Fishwick's, and the Victoria Arms pub.

By way of a change, the inside of a building is shown here. The sign in this shop says, 'Mr Therm's Kitchen'. This was the Gas Showrooms of the 1950s. There are some interesting items for sale, such as wringers at 84 shillings (£4.20) and dolly tubs.

In 1958, a traffic census took place in Pall Mall. In those days it was a wide road, free from obstructions. You could turn right without holding up traffic behind you and you didn't need to brake suddenly due to emerging traffic coming blindly out of side streets.

Into Moor Road in the 1950s. These Chorley Colliery miners' cottages were still in use across the road from the petrol station. The colliery yard itself was behind the cottages.

Now to Lyons Lane in the mid-1950s, at its junction with Standish Street and Brook Street. This view is taken looking towards Brown's Mill, (Chortex) and Lyons Lane Bridge. Note the old cottages on the left, and the pub beyond. This was the Castle Inn.

Looking the other way in Lyons Lane, from the Castle Inn (to right), towards Standish Street. The tall building above the old cottages was one of the earliest mills in Chorley, started by Timothy Lightoller.

Just before Lyons Lane Bridge, close to the railway line, stood this row of old cottages until 1958 or so. Its official name was Whittles Court, but it was known under a more derogatory name.

One of the streets off Bolton Road was Queen Street East. Today, its location can be ascertained due to the factory chimney above the cottages, which the author had a hand in preserving. The old cottages were former weavers' cottages, demolished in 1958.

Out of town for this building. Today this scene is only a memory, its site has been made into a 'consolidated' ruin. This was Clayton Hall in 1958.

Out of Chorley town again, but not too far with this view. It is Higher Burgh Hall, photographed by the author during the later 1950s. This hall is yet another building, which has been demolished.

SPORTING DAYS

This early 1950s photograph shows Chorley FC supporters in Duke Street entering Victory Park to watch a League Cup game.

At that cup match, Victory Park was full to capacity, as can be seen from the above photograph. Everyone seems to be wearing a raincoat and most are in caps or trilby hats.

Another group of supporters at Chorley FC's ground, thought to be photographed around 1954. There are several lady supporters and not a hint of trouble. One wonders how everyone managed to see the action, though.

Young fans crammed into Victory Park, with a few slightly older faces. One supporter has gone to great lengths with that striped topper.

A not-too-happy looking crowd emerge from Victory Park at the Ashby Street exit, on to Duke Street which is still cobbled.

Chorley FC first team pictured in 1958 in front of the grandstand at their Victory Park ground.

For local cricket fans of the 1950s, this was the Chorley team they supported. Players (back row, left to right) are: J. Andrew, T. Norman, O. Demming, C. Dixon, F. Henry, B. Ellison. Front: J. Lancaster, T. Dugdale, A. Mockett (captain), J. Pomfret, E. Donaldson.

Surely one of the most scenic cricket grounds in the county is that used by the White Coppice team in the 1950s. Here, Mr Smith is receiving a trophy and another face familiar to many people will be that of Mr Farnworth, to the right.

These two photographs show the Chorley and District Midweek Cricket League champions Whittle-le-Woods, above, and the Rest of the League select side who they met in a challenge match, shown below.

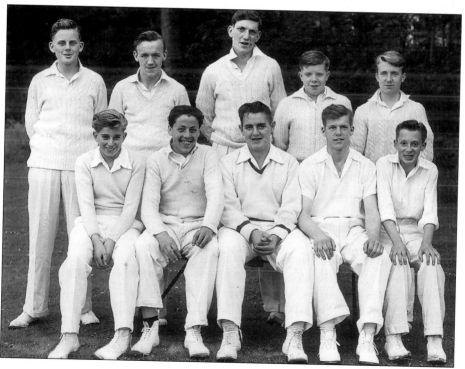

Now it is the turn of the Corinthians Hockey Club, pictured here on Astley Park in the 1950s.

The Corinthians again. Back row (left to right) are: Barbara Wilson, Brenda Jolly, Marion Pearce, Margaret Wells, Jean Bennison, Mavis Roberts. Front row: Doreen Jackson, Marina Bell, Dorothea Calderbank, Sylvia Bennison, Evick Critchley.

Hockey players take time off as well – and here's proof of that. Pictured at one of the Corinthians' annual dances, thought to be in the Tudor Ballroom, are members of the team and their friends, all contemporaries of the author.

A varied group of sportsmen, including, in the centre, kneeling, Alan Hunt, British champion weightlifter from Chorley. The author was at Hollinshead Street School with Alan. His father had a dental practice in Clifford Street. Many will also know Mick McGreal, standing, second from left.

Bowling is as popular today as it was in the 1950s, although there are fewer greens in Chorley than 60 years ago. This 1958 photograph was taken at East Ward Club, on President's Day. Among those present are Mr and Mrs Clarke and Mr E. Pilkington.

Another local bowling club, pictured with their trophy in the 1950s.

The Dispatch Cycle Rally passed through Euxton in the 1950s. The first photograph shows cyclists passing the Bay Horse which seems to be under repair or alteration. The second photograph shows them passing Euxton Lane End, where houses have been built today.

This photograph was taken outside the Bridge Inn at Botany. It appears to be a group of anglers having participated in a competition, probably on the canal adjoining. Holding the cup is another contemporary of the author, Dennis Spedding. The shop and houses next to the pub are now demolished.

For several years, certainly through the war till the 1950s, aeroplanes were built and stored in Chorley. These were used by the Moss Brothers in international air races. The planes were kept at the Varnish and Paint Works, Crook Street. They were called 'Mosscraft'.

PERSONAL NOTES

Like so many others from Chorley, the author and his friends often went to Butlin's holiday camps, as they were called then, Pwllheli and Filey being particularly popular. On this 1955 photograph, at Filey, are (left to right) Bob Catterall, Brian Ditchfield, the author and Brian Ogden.

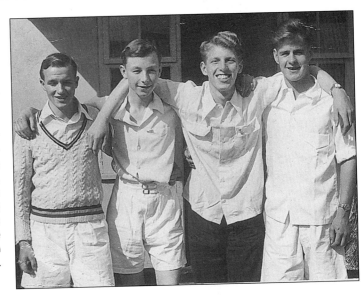

A year or so later, it was holiday time again and this time the destination was the Isle of Man. Here, about to leave from Farrington Street, are Eric Halton, John Sellars, Brian Ogden and the author. The houses to the left were used by police.

The later 1950s saw the author spend much less time in Chorley after he joined the Merchant Navy as engineer officer on a passenger ship on the Australia run, where he kept up with local news through Chorley folk in 'Oz'. Photographed here in Sydney on RMS *Strathmore*.

The early 1960s saw the author on other ships running around the coast of India, to China and the Phillippines, plus troopship service.